history of a nation of one

jecon gregory

history
of a nation
# of one

harcourt, brace & world, inc., new york

to my next of kin—
Adam

in the beginning...

Harcourt, Brace & World, Inc.
757 Third Avenue
New York, N.Y. 10017

Dear Sirs,

Enclosed please find parts of the manuscript of *History of a Nation of One* by Jecon Gregory, together with postage for its return if necessary. He wishes it to be considered for publication. I have typed it and am willing to receive your reply, since Jecon himself has no fixed address.

I should explain that he is a person of about thirty, very tall and thin, reticent and melancholy, and a pure nomad. He walks, has no shoes, pulls all his possessions in a basket on wheels, sleeps in a tent, and makes his living by knocking at doors and drawing people's portraits in pastel. He has wandered all over Europe, North Africa, and Western Asia, and has come by way of Iceland to North America. He has been living in this and similar ways for around twenty years. It is uncertain where he was born or even what his original language was, since he lost his home at an early age; the first country he remembers is Malta. . . .

principal contents

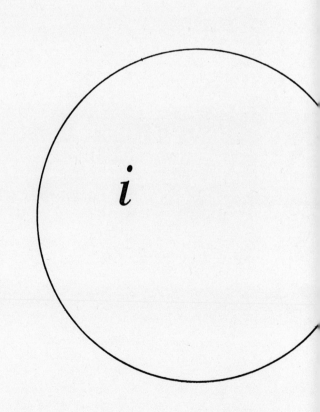

i

O lover, when they kill me
Will you know what to say,
What to scream at the motorist
As he hurtles on his way?

Before he's out of earshot
How, lover, will you sum
The seven books I'm writing
And the eight that are to come?

How will that motorist
By your third word or your fourth
Understand your body
Is widowed like the north?

Learn this curse, lover,
Get it ready to be hurled:
"Motorist, O motorist,
You have killed the world."

serendib

I had fallen into a crevasse, I was lying on my back, and I was looking up at the moon. It was at zenith, and its shape was a D.

What did that mean?

It meant that this moment was sunset. The night would soon fall. Cold would come to my crevasse, licking my sweat. I shut my eyes again.

I could not move, because several parts of me were full of a pain that waited only to be rattled. I let my hand grip the ground I was lying on. It was damp gravel. When I next opened my eyes, the moon had gone. So I looked at the walls of the crevasse. They were bushes of sicklethorn. I studied my environment. Gradually I accepted that the daylight was not waning but increasing.

What did that mean?

It meant that the moon was north of me, and I was in the Southern Hemisphere.

Actually I was not in the Southern Hemisphere, but in Ceylon. It was winter; the sun being in Capricorn, the full moon, opposite to it, rides on the Tropic of Cancer. I don't say I worked all this out just then. However, I remembered I was in Ceylon. I had been sleeping on the beach, and a crowd of small men robbed me of everything except these swimming trunks.

I thought of what had been in my bag. A block made from a scraper-board drawing, the metal going moldy. A genealogical tree of Homeric heroes, four feet long. A hat, which I used only for carrying eggs. A paraffin burner for which I had once paid half a crown. Two misbegotten screws, without slots in their heads. A card showing my blood group. And a dried long-tailed leaf of the peepul, the Bo tree of Buddha's enlightenment; only its net of veins left, and on them the souvenir man had painted not Buddha but Christ and some sheep.

What among these had made me try to fight back? Must be getting older—more attached to property. I did not like to think how the blow which knocked me out had not been to the head.

Instead I thought about *serene, selene, serenade, seren-dipity*. Serendipity is finding things you weren't looking for. But it happens only when the mind is prepared for some discovery or other. The *Three Princes of Serendib* (which is Ceylon) kept bumping into things they weren't looking for. I tried to think of an example of serendipity. At length I remembered one: Senefelder wrote a laundry list for his mother on a piece of slate with a greasy pencil —discovered lithography.

I summoned my tendons to begin raising a limb. I got up and walked to Mannar. I made the police at each place responsible for getting me to the next. At Anuradhapura I met a German professor and twenty students, who gave me a wallet full of Deutsche marks, thinking they could not change them here. On the very last stage of the journey into Colombo I was on top of a lorry with a crowd of other people; the wallet slipped out of my belt and a man seized it, jumped off, and swiftly vanished. Nobody would believe me when I told them *both* my strokes of misfortune.

toy island

I ran away from home when I was small and I could never find it again. I begged sweets from a sweetshop, and was fed by children till they got tired of my crying. I don't know what language they and I spoke. The first locality I remember is Malta.

There I had been taken by Olive and Finlaw. They meant to look after me, but when they were not fighting the Hun they were at parties. I hardly ever saw Olive out of her sharp Wrens uniform. Sliema, the English town, had a grey straight sea front, as in any Sussex resort, and rows of houses called "Norma," "Iris," or "My Nest," instead of "Christ the King," "Viva Kristu Re," or "Casa San Duminku," as elsewhere on the island. I used to lie on the rocks till some family let me play with their children and then took me home to tea; or I went to St. Julian's Bay, climbed and hid in half-bombed buildings, tried to steal boats which had eyes painted on their prows, fell out of a window embrasure straight into Marsa Mxett Harbour and was stung by the jellyfish that teemed in it. My language was Malti tal-Mama, the Maltese of Sliema, where they affect English and Italian words like *mama* instead of *omm*. People called to me: "Don't throw stones —you might hit your own father!"

Olive went on leave to Alexandria, where she came from. I was put in the Vernon Institute on top of the ramparts of Valletta. I longed to own a locker like others in the Institute; I couldn't unless someone bought me a padlock to put on it (though I had nothing to keep inside it). Finlaw didn't doubt I was independent enough to come to him on his days off, over Marsa Mxett on one of the *dghajsas*, little bright gondolas rowed by standing men who face forward and push crossed oars tied to the rowlocks. But I couldn't find my way down to the water. I got lost in the barracks and courtyards of Floriana. I was scared by the sobbing noise of a stonecutter's saw (a noise that visitors to Malta often take for a donkey's bray, but there are no donkeys). Then someone started shooting pigeons in a church; the tremendous volleying made me think an air raid was on, and I had no shelter to go to. I tried again after dark; the pigeon-shooting broke out again (it is quite a regular occurrence), now accompanied by flares of light. I tried again next day, and finally found the quayside. It was in the wrong place for the *dghajsas*, but the road along the water's edge began to tell its narrative and my feet began to listen.

I followed the edge of Pietà Creek and the edge of Msida Creek and at last climbed into open country. But soon came another town (Birkirkara). Then another (Lija), on a slight hill. The road passed round its walls, and divided round its cemetery, a small walled oval with a chapel in the middle. Then I turned so many corners that I lost my sense of direction. I noticed a street shrine I had already seen; so I had gone round in a circle and was heading back. I accepted that, and spent the night in the garden of San Antonio Palace. In the morning I wandered into Attard, where a miniature bypass called Street of the Notary Zarb becomes involved with the town wall and the blocky buildings and irregular lanes on the edge of the town. This is the kind of urban scenery that set my taste. I sat on a bench with a pleasant view toward

Zebbug, till a *carrozzi* stopped by me. "Valletta," I said; "do you know where that is?" I feared I might be in an enemy country—perhaps even Italy—and was relieved that the man understood Maltese.

A convoy was in port, the Institute was crowded, there were dances and smoking-concerts, I was in a dormitory with the sailors. Then I had a cabin of my own, with no windows, but the window in the corridor outside looked out over Floriana, which is like a masonry flag, made less of houses than of monuments and parade grounds; bounded by its own great mesh of landward ramparts. Now I didn't spend every night inside; though I was scolded by Bursar or Matron, they could see that what they said didn't apply. I woke among the scented trees in the Argotti Gardens on top of a bastion, looking down over tier on tier of fortifications, across to the uptilted panorama of limestone blotched with white towns, and far away at the top a huge square palace and a city sailing out more notably than all the others. I asked a sailor at the window what those places were and whether the places I had reached were nearer or farther; he didn't know, of course. Through the thin partitions I heard sailors in other cubicles discussing their evenings in the Gut:

"That's it, then—I've been robbed!" Or:

"Oh, I was just playing with her behind. . . ."

The promenade of everybody up and down Kingsway, from Kingsgate to Palace Square and back again, all vehicles excluded, went on from eight o'clock till nine. Beyond Palace Square, down into the dark seaward end of the town; squads of Navy and Air Force police disappearing into the turnings that led to the Gut, officially Strait Street. Strait indeed: while I was picking my way along the middle, a girl standing in a doorway could grab me round the waist. I struggled and a crowd gathered. She dragged me inside, the crowd followed, and I had to wrestle with her on the stage. She pinned me again and again.

I hung around this "Ark Royal Bar, By Joseph Gauci" (as if it was a book); I was not exactly on the staff, though there was a plan to make me Cupid in a tableau. I was fed (though too much with tomato juice and vodka) and besieged by "brown-booters," and I sat on the doorstep among fat old women, gramophone music, frying smells, and groaning sailors.

A man came in, wearing black trousers and white socks, and getting a bit of paper out of his pocket (which he did to make us think he was in the middle of some work). He was Grundy, who was supposed to manage the bar and the accounts, and he was late as usual.

I asked somebody, "Why does he wear a black tie?"

"So we'll be kind to him. It should be a black armband anyway, but he pretends he's English. Everyone knows his name is really Grandi."

There were also Santa, who occupied most of the stage, and Prosper, who played the banjo and carried the crates, and who thought I should not have to sleep on a window sill. So I was taken home to his family in Senglea. We got on the Grand Harbour ferry; beside us on the quay sailors queued for *dghajsas* to take them to their ships.

From the man-made crags of Valletta—the maze of immense strongholds, the "Cavaliers" of St. John and St. James, ditches cut down to sea level, staired streets, alleys crossing each other by bridges or diving behind churches, doors and windows opening in improbable places, the gardens which top the Upper and Lower Barrakkas and are themselves topped by roofless arches, and the elevator that goes up two hundred feet inside the moat—the preoc-

/ 10

cupying view all the time is the three older cities across the harbour: Vittoriosa and Senglea like battleships nosing outward (Fort Saint Angelo on the tip of Vittoriosa actually ranks as a battleship, and Senglea is still known to the people as L'Isla) and star-shaped Cospicua at their base. Already they were half ruined, but Senglea was still a narrow mass of tall tenements rising flush with the rock and penetrated by only a few canyon-like streets.

As you approach Senglea over the water, you see caves open in the rock at the water's level. Inside them, steps run up into the city. And there are the tunnels where the people went when the sirens sounded. Beside the harbour a *dghajsa*, drawn up on the cobbles, had been holed by a bomb, so that the remaining prow and walls of the boat looked like some ornamental exit from a well. Almost touching it with a wing tip lay the ruins of a Junker dive bomber. Ramps of rubble mounted so high around some houses that only the fourth and fifth stories showed—and people lived in them. St. Heaven Street was so mountainous with blocks bigger than men that people had established a route through someone's gate, up a rubble slope over a wall, through the shell of what had been a house, and out by another wrought-iron gate. The great church of St. Victory was shattered like a nut by a hammer, with everything sliding into the crypt. The side of an aisle, a mountain range of vast carved architecture, had keeled outward, but lay supported at a slope by already fallen rubble, which now under its weight was being ground to chalk.

Bells rang—perhaps for the elevation of the Host in a nearby church, and then people stopped talking and knelt in the street—and if it wasn't a bell it was a siren starting up. But they wailed so often that no one bothered to go to earth till a sailor hoisted the red flag, "enemy aircraft near," on the signal roof in Valletta, or the dockyard alert sounded in Cospicua. Then some went under the arches of ramparts and bridges, some into rock shelters at the foot of cliffs just outside the fortifications, and we found our way from the houses down into the tunnels, and came to an enormous underground room. It was like a railway station, its walls and ceiling a single arch. Square wooden frames stood in long lines, planks resting across them, bedding and belongings and people on the planks. Some were two-decker, some three, and between these higher structures were slung the paraffin lamps that gave us light. Children raced around the aisles and clambered, and knocked ladders down, so that the arched volume of air beat like a heart. When everyone was still, those next to the wall could hear the rock creak or grunt.

Every fever in later childhood led to one same dream: the vaulted underground shelter in Malta had become an immense Crystal Palace under the sea. The floor, like the vault, was glass. I had to travel along it down monstrous steps. From the edge of each step I had to leap across a pool of poison that occupied the nearer part of the next step. And if I hesitated too long, the glass broke and I fell through into the poison, for it also extended back under the step I was on. The succession of steps was almost infinite, but not quite. At the end of the glass palace there was always a red bus waiting to take me to Birmingham.

Mrs. Micallef began to worry that somebody had shut a window she had left open. . . . She had hung blankets at the windows to catch glass, and she had opened the windows in case of shock, but she thought she remembered seeing someone shut a window again. . . .

And when we came out after the all-clear, we found the

house gone. The whole row gone. They were cleft from top to bottom like a cake. In the standing part we could see the pictures on the walls of people's rooms up to the sixth floor. A carpet hung over a floor joist. At the top a thin pile of stone blocks balanced against the sky. A multiple window frame without any glass in it dangled from one screw. A wall stood folded across the middle— lower half leaning out, top half leaning in—ready to descend.

Wardens and children were picking over the rubble; other people just sat on a parapet in the sunshine. A priest had come in case there were any deaths. Prosper began pulling his bed out and taking it to pieces and tying it on a cart. I wandered back round the harbour. There were two other raids while I was on my way—they used to come a dozen a day sometimes. At the Vernon Institute they had assumed I was dead.

But no one had time to watch over a Sliema orphan or bastard or whatever I was. Once I lay out on the roof of Ta-Liesse Church near the Grand Harbour (where I had lain to bask in the day) and saw the ack-ack stains on the sky, and the huge trees of spray and smoke and fire that went up from bombs hitting the water. Waves of concussion knocked dustbins along the street. Masonry fell slowly in formations like mattresses, bounced, sank again, bounced again but this time looser; and then white dust puffed from under it and enveloped me so that I could not breathe except through a dampened corner of my shirt.

A convoy came in led by a ship whose side was peppered with holes and plugged with bits of wood. The *Illustrious*, an aircraft carrier, crept into the Grand Harbour crippled and on fire, to be repaired at the dockyard. From then till the *Illustrious* slipped out to Alexandria, German

/ 13

dive bombers lashed French Creek, and the destruction spread to the Three Cities close around—Vittoriosa, Cospicua, and Senglea, but most of all Senglea. Senglea had been the most densely populated place in Europe; afterward, it was not.

One day I met a boy called Mannerwell diving for shrapnel, and he took me home to his house in Our Lady of Sorrows Street, Hamrun. A man happened to come collecting the family's weekly contribution of threepence for whenever the town could next hold a *festa*, and when he heard about me he said he would bring the policeman and we would find my people. I left by a window which opened onto a roof.

Beyond Hamrun's mile-long main street, the road followed a slight ridge beside the old aqueduct of Grand Master Wignacourt. The aqueduct had become a mere wall between fields by the blocking up of most of the arches, and I slept under one of them. Only a few hundred yards beyond this aqueduct, a continuous spread of brown roofs filled the shallow valley alongside—Birkirkara and the Three Villages (Balzan, Lija, and Attard). Next day I walked up the steep road slanting into Rabat. On my right was that shining little city I had often seen on the horizon from down in Valletta: Mdina, the ancient capital, projecting on a rock cut off by a moat from the now larger Rabat.

Children were begging pennies from sight-seers, and I wondered whether to join them. Then an elderly gentleman took me for a walk. He wore a hat, a red corduroy coat, and blue trousers, and carried a violin case. He guided me round Mdina all morning. The labyrinthine alleys were viscous with incredible peace, the great buildings creamed with something thicker than light. My guide pointed out those that were Norman and those that were Roman, and the houses of the old noble families (among them his own), and the grating through which the Benedictine monks still received their supplies. We emerged on the ramparts at the chin of the hill and looked at a panorama of Malta. We counted thirty-three towns and villages, among them Pawla, conspicuous because its grid of streets was oriented toward us.

The old man suggested lunch in the "English Gwest-House." But I pretended I'd have to go home now and come again in the afternoon, and I walked away uphill.

Rabat ended; open country tending upward; a little village (Dingli), and then a lane, which seemed about to come to an end, and nothing else but the horizon and the sun slung over it. It seemed to me that my conscious life had really begun, and that ahead of me lay the infinity of the world, without towns, without the exertions of being bombed, without roads, lanes, or paths—nothing but stones and the carob trees, whose pods I knew how to eat. And then suddenly I came to the brink of a cliff, eight hundred feet high. Beyond was nothing but sea, bending to Africa.

I drifted back along the lane till the spires and domes of Rabat, glowing orange in the evening sun, pricked over the horizon ahead of me. The landscape around me seemed habitable: instead of walls there were low cliffs, six feet high or less, surrounding irregular depressions like pools of soft plowed earth. These were quarries, disused and filled in. One hollow contained big crates of food, tea, and gin, with stones piled over them as camouflage from enemy aircraft. In one of the low cliffs I found the entrance to a catacomb half buried.

The night became cold and I got up and moved on into the town. When the sun rose I saw a bridge above me: I was in the moat between Rabat and Mdina, where Malta's disused railway line runs. I went in through the Bieb il-Griegi, the Gate of the Greeks. I hoped to see the beauties of the city by myself. But the gentleman with red corduroy coat, blue trousers, and violin case was there again as if to meet me, and we resumed our tour. I wondered why an old man who looked prosperous should spend all day apparently in the hope of earning a shilling tip from a child.

Old man: "You like wandering about away from home, do you?"

I: "Oh, no!"

Soon, as he seemed unconvinced, I added, "I don't know why everybody is always changing places."

The old man said: "You know what Gahan told the person who asked him why it is that every morning all the people leave their houses and go in different directions?"

"No."

"Gahan said: 'Because if they all went in the same direction, the earth would lose its balance and turn turtle.'"

This is one of those thousands of anecdotes, profounder than they seem, from Malta's Arabic centuries. Their sage-fool hero is he who is called in Sicily Giufà or Giucà; in Calabria, Hiohà or Juvadi; in Berber-land, Si Jeha or Shaha; in Egypt, Guha; in Syria, Nasreddin Effendi Juha; above all, in Turkey and throughout the Balkans, Nasreddin the Khoja.

We went into the cathedral and he showed me pictures by Caravaggio, Raphael, and St. Luke; a fantastic altarpiece by Guido Reni; painted ceilings; high altar of lapis lazuli and now unobtainable marbles; floors like Persian carpets; pictures that are of inlaid wood, but one discovers it only on feeling them; medallions that look like oil paintings till one stands where the light reflects off them and sees that they are upright mosaics of tiny stones. The old man told me how Caravaggio joined the Knights of Malta after having to flee from Italy when he killed a man in a duel, and how Mattia Preti, decorator of the Co-Cathedral in Valletta, was expelled from the Order for *nearly* killing a man in the same way. I asked whether all artists have to fight.

The end of the afternoon came. I said I had no money to tip him with. He got out of me where I had come from. He took me to Sliema and knocked on the door of Olive's apartment. He asked if he might take me out sometimes. Olive sharply said no. As he was going away, he went to a square nearby and sat on a bench playing his violin.

I made what I called an "epic" to tell Olive where I had been.

> When I started moving
> Songs became possible.
> It was ten o'clock in the morning.
> My head went along high and low in the air.
> I passed through Floriana,
> I passed through Hambrun.
> I borrowed some gloves
> And lived on the prickly pear. . . .

Olive said, "Composing poetry is more difficult than you think," and she put me through a course of English verse, mostly Goldsmith. She said, "I want you to try writing a diary in rhyme, describing everywhere you go. You can write a bit of it each day. If you do it all your life, that *will* be an epic." So, laboriously, I produced stuff like:

. . . Tea taken, for an evening stroll we went,
On Floriana's exploration bent.
The central avenue, Il Mall—the court,
Like London's Pall Mall, for an ancient sport—
And that wide space named from the granaries
Which litter it—called "fosos" in Maltese—
Set off the parish church, a massive pile,
Not less than Westminster's in size or style.
Its bells, whose noise some rail at, are not rung
By lengthy ropes, but have their clappers swung. . . .

Olive said to Finlaw: "We never take the kid anywhere. No wonder he runs away. You must spend your day off taking him for a bus ride." So Finlaw donned his shorts; his bald kneecaps amid hairy legs twinkled whitely like two smudges of chalk.

He took me to the valley garden of the Boschetto, where the people carouse through the night before the Feast of Saints Peter and Paul; another time, to Marsaxlokk, the little port where everyone picnics after the great cross-island procession of St. Gregory in April, whence we walked by a cart track over the cliffs past St. Thomas's Tower, the reef of the Munxaghr or "saw," and some fish-ponds, to Marsascala. Another afternoon, to the opposite end of the island, where we bathed at Monk's Cove in St. Paul's Bay, and again—despite shoals of flotsam—in the cold though shallow waters of Mellieha Bay. Between the two bays the road, before it climbs to Mellieha on the hilltop, dips into an unexpected green slit, the Wied tal Mistra. "I would sleep here," I said suddenly to Finlaw. He stopped the bus, and we got out and went to lie on a patch of grass and flowers. It was infested with camel ticks. "You see!" he said. We walked up to that most imposing of the village towns, Mellieha, with its cliffside shrine marked out by splashes of maroon paint and a great statue of the Virgin (the occupant before her was the nymph Calypso).

Two young girls sat on a bench beside the road; one of them wore a bridesmaid's dress.

"Please ask her why she's wearing that," said Finlaw.

So I went to them and opened my mouth to speak, but the other girl immediately silenced me with a gesture.

"I know what it is," said Finlaw as we walked on. "She's almost blind, and doesn't even know she put the wedding dress on today. And her friend doesn't want her to know, because there's a superstition that if you put a wedding dress on by mistake you'll be married soon, but if you notice your mistake you never will. Do you know how I fell in love with Olive? It was my school sports day, and she noticed that I had odd socks on. She went round making sure nobody told me, and so I won the hop-skip-and-jump and the four-forty, whereas if I'd have known about it I would have come last.

"When we were married," continued Finlaw, "the bridesmaids carried white staffs. People hurried out of the pews to help them—thought they were blind!"

Another day he took me and his snorkel to the Blue Grotto of Zurrieq. The road forked and forked through a landscape that was the balks between innumerable square chunks cut out by quarries. Finlaw was still talking about his wedding. He claimed that when you say "With all my worldly goods I thee endow," you are allowed to insert any one item. So he and Olive agreed to say "With all my worldly goods and my whole walnuts I thee endow." For it is almost impossible to get a walnut out of its shell whole.

In Mqabba the bus gets through the narrowest streets buses can get through; backs down a lane to reach Qrendi, where there is nowhere to turn round. Here we got out to walk. These little towns seem larger than they are because it is so hard to follow directions through the tortuous streets that pierce them. While we were trying to find our way out of Qrendi, we heard some chilling shrieks. Finlaw stopped and clutched me by my ear, saying, "Don't you ever run away again, my lad." We took a path that led to the edge of a pit, a hundred and thirty feet deep, called the Makluba. "You see," said Finlaw, "the countryside just isn't safe for you. That madwoman we heard just now, screaming—" "It was a parrot in a house," I said. But he wouldn't believe me.

The road broke through to the coast, and framed in the gap we saw Filfla, a crag four miles out to sea. It used to grow pepper, as its name means, but now it was a target for firing practice. Two planes dived at it, and puffs of smoke went up from it. A red flag on a tower showed when Filfla was being peppered. The road, curling steeply down past the tower and half a dozen houses, ended as a slipway into the Wied iz Zurrieq. This winding lane of water penetrated the mountainside between walls of what seemed not real rock, but rock in a pen-and-ink drawing. A fisherman took the block from under a boat and slid it into the water, and rowed us round to the bay where another valley ends. But it ends suspended on high cliffs, where fig trees grow not merely from vertical rock, but from overhanging rock. Deep water swayed against the legs of rock arches. We sailed through them and along the caves. Turquoise blue illuminated the water when we looked against the light. We chased it but did not catch it. It writhed against the foot of the rock; in one cave it filled the water to the brim, and the oar generated shoals of brilliant bubbles. I waited for Finlaw to take his swim, but he was unnerved, and I took the snorkel instead and got over the side of the boat. The grottoes were not at all eerie above water, but the water went down so deep, and was so airlike in its clarity, I had transferred myself to the ceiling of fearful chasms. I tried to seem unconcerned, but kept close to the boat and the surface and moved out toward the sunlight. There I took the snorkel off and handed it back as if there was no more to see under-water, and swam with my head up, trying not to think of the caves and arches and plunging slopes below me and the things that might emerge from them. I swam under the cliff. A steam roller, smoothing a road along the top of it, plied to and fro on the sky line. Suddenly Finlaw shouted to me and tried to make the boatman row out. He had caught sight of a mass of soft gravel and rubble which he thought was on the point of shaking out of the cliff on our heads. It was really granite, oddly weathered. "Let me get back to something safe like fighting the Germans," said Finlaw as I climbed into the boat. He took no interest when the boatman cheated us of four shillings.

Children swirled in very rough games among the fallen blocks of stone in the Manderaggio, the dense quarter in a dent made by ancient quarrying on the north side of Valletta. We struck walls or fell on hard ground without taking any notice of the bruises. We dressed ourselves as Boy Scouts and tried to sell postcards in aid of our "jam-boree"; the postcards were already written on, and we wondered why they wouldn't sell. Proper Maltese *festas*— with the greasy poles, masks, horse races, masked penitents dragging chains from their ankles, men carrying the figure of Christ uphill at a run, and, above all, the fireworks—were generally impossible because of the air-raid warnings, but nevertheless we were always letting off fireworks, on the stone lids of the *fosos*, in the tethering holes in walls, under neighbors' wives' skirts. A man started up his car; it wailed; the bystanders knew quite well that when he lifted the hood he would find a firework attached to the wires. Many of the boys of twelve—and they seemed big men to me—were bus conductors, especially on Sundays. We would go and play inside the idle buses at the bus station on the rampart. Each had its own illuminated shrine beside the driver's seat. Quarreling over chocolate bars that sailors had given us, we asked a man to share them out, and he said, "Shall I do it as man would, or as God would?" And we answered, "As man would!" For we knew the story of Gahan, in which the children piously answer, "As God would!" and so to some he gives many nuts, to others none at all.

A child called to me: "I know how old you are. You're eight."

"No, I'm not."

"Nine."

"Wrong."

"Seven."

"Wrong."

"Six."

"Wrong."

"Five."

"Wrong."

"Four."

"Wrong."

"You're eight!"

"No, I'm not."

"Nine."

"Wrong."

"Ten."

"Wrong."

"Eleven."

"Wrong."

"Twelve."

"Wrong."

"Thirteen."

"Wrong."

"Fourteen."

"Wrong."

"Fifteen."

"Wrong."

"What are you then?"

"Sixteen."

People were running past the end of the street. We ran with them. We came to a waste plot near the Lazaretto Creek where a plane had crashed. One propeller stuck up like an oar, the black cross painted on it. A young man lay back on the wreckage, his gauntleted hand raised and his dead head near the blaze. He had brown hair and a small beard, and I saw he had been something of a wit (in his native German).

Il Belt—The City, Valletta—is really a huge castle sectioned by streets. Now all the interconnected showpieces were gone, or seemed so as their own ruin mounted around them.

The great law courts, the central point of the city, had become like the pad of grey ash at the center of a burnt-out fire. The Opera House, too solid to fall down, was ground from above by bombs till it was a stump, topped with the white snow of its own debris. The Argotti Gardens, with their squat palms and round pools overlooked by colonnades, had tilted and shaken into one slide of rubble. Stones from the façade and architrave of San Publiju, the huge parish church of Floriana, became a horizontal layer over the plaza in front of it, and men pushed them aside to hoist sacks of grain out of the *fosos* underneath. A bomb passed plumb through the roadway of the Porte Reale Bridge, the main way into Valletta. Walking round the hole to get across, you peered at its stratified sides, like a pit cut through chalky soil. From the moat underneath, you looked up at the patch of bright sunlight on the pier of the arch. There was a jetty at the mouth of the Grand Harbour: bombs severed it from the land, and I thought it would float away. (The gap has been found advantageous and is permanent.)

What seemed like something thorny growing out of the dust heaps was warped pieces of wrought-iron balustrades torn from the Auberges of the Knights. It wasn't like being in a town any more, where you have to keep to the public channels of streets between the opaque, secret houses. Now you could sometimes see clear across or through the blocks to right and left, but not along the street ahead. It was like a jungle, where you could move any way with varying difficulty. Glancing down as you went, you might see a man with a pipe and hat and his hands in his pockets, slouching through the sunny basement of his house, calmly looking for something. One of the steep stepped streets had become an avalanche of blocks, towering up to the notch of sky at the top; mixed with it, fallen shop signs, laundry which had been strung across the street, the arm of the Queen of Heaven from a corner shrine; and at the bottom of the avalanche stood someone's little dolly cart, as if it were going to take all this weight. People, holding perhaps a can of water in one hand and a roll of clothes under the other arm, stood balancing on rocks as if they were scrambling at the seaside, testing the next one with a toe to see if it was steady. In the middle of a street you would come on a place where the rubble opened out, the white ground was swept, the chipped blocks had retreated into orderly square piles with corrugated iron laid across them, and a man and three women and nine children were laughing about something as they squatted round a fry pan.

A deep moat continues the slope of Floriana's rampart down into the rock. Along the base of it, every few yards, there are entrances to catacombs. One raid, I was taken into one of them.

There are caves and catacombs under the surface of Malta wherever there are buildings on top. They connected palaces, they led from the Knights' headquarters to fortifications, they came up behind the lines of besieging enemies. Or they were dwellings of the Phoenicians, graves, underground temples. Or they led to wells and cisterns; tunnels were driven along the water table to collect water, and lately tunnels had been driven along a lower water table at sea level, and it was said that the sea was coming in. There is no water on Malta except underground, and I remember my astonishment later on seeing streams.

Now people were living in rock shelters opening out from quarries at the mouths of the catacombs, or even deeper, in the catacombs themselves. And there was not enough room for the refugees, and British soldiers and Maltese in gangs were cutting more. And there were not enough picks to cut the rock with, and the dockyard forges were set to making more.

While we were still in the cave we heard the Angelus ring, and we stood in a circle while a man read a prayer in a piping nasal voice. It was Grundy, who used to keep the books in the Ark Royal Bar. He had developed a sad mannerism: every now and then, he let a look as of pain cross his face. It was because of his fear of unkindness.

He told me he had volunteered for war work and had been loading ammunition belts for Spitfires. But he had stopped that and was now clerking in a government department. Prosper's nephew Ninu was in the same department. Prosper, with his family, had been evacuated to the country. They had gone, as the town members of a family often do, to work with the country members on the family farm.

Now the government department itself had been bombed, and they were forced to put up some temporary quarters in a field. As is the law whenever a field in little Malta is built on, the topsoil had to be carted out into the country and used to make a disused quarry into a new field.

"We're taking a ride on the lorry with Ninu," said Grundy. "It's going down near to where his people are."

I and Ninu and Grundy and Grundy's infant daughter, Denise, presented ourselves with a ground sheet to lay on top of the dirt, but the lorry driver said, "Want to sit on compost and sludge, do you? That's what we're picking up at Luqa." He found room for all of us in his cabin, except Ninu, who was big and had to cling somewhere outside. We passed the Marsa race track and stopped near the military airport, untidy and shabby. Here we had to add to the scrapings of the field a load of urban refuse—for that too by law must be used in the making of new fields. While they were shoveling it aboard, I stood on the roof of the cabin and looked over the airfield. It was at this moment that it occurred to me to think: "I love every yard of this land." An English child is nostalgic about the details of his native fragment of a county. Malta is only two thirds the size of the Isle of Wight, and is a complete antique nation. You cannot widen a road—or even pave a road—without breaking someone's heart. Yet there are three airfields, besides many other military playgrounds, and a racecourse occupying the only plain. When the Italians started altering Malta from the air, it is not surprising that the Italianate period in Malta was concluded, and the dispute as to second language—Italian or English —came to rest.

We drove on by winding lanes of hard white earth like ice. Prosper and nearly a dozen of his relatives and the farmer joined us with a hamper of food and several bottles of wine, and we sat picknicking beside the hole we had just filled with our refuse. Because of what that refuse included, we were not free from flies. There was a view of Cala San Jorj and Pretty Bay, and Birzebbuga between them, all oil tanks and pipelines.

The farmer was an excessively shriveled old man. As he sat in the shade, there was at his back a small cliff stained bronze, and a bush overhead. And there was a recess like the top of a cave now mostly refilled by the ground. "Where does that go to?" I asked him. "To Valletta," he said.

"No, it goes nowhere," he admitted when pressed. "But there is a way into the caves near here that goes all the way to Valletta."

"We should go home that way!" said Grundy.

So, led by the ancient man, Prosper and Ninu and Grundy and Grundy's daughter and I set off in single file along a contour path, beside a hedge formed of the bats of prickly pears. There were crickets in the corn upslope, heaps of sulla in the field below. Someone meanwhile ran to the farmer's house for candles.

Were we really going all the way to Valletta underground? Even if the tunnel went all the seven miles, perhaps we would have come up around the Wied Dalam, which lay in the way. Its floor was then being covered with installations leading to underground petrol tanks, and in its side was one of the greatest of Maltese caves, the Ghar Dalam, full of prehistoric bones, but now the R.A.F. were storing petrol in it too, and the fumes were making patterns on the ceiling.

Not far inside our cave, the old man pointed out branches that led to St. Lucien's Tower on Ras Qrejten, to Dowdall's Hotel and the gun batteries. He spoke singsong, breaking his speech into short lengths of which he drew out the first syllable and then rattled through the rest. This tunnel and its connections totaled, he said, thirty-two known miles. He had lived here for thirty-five years and not seen half of it.

By stamping on the floor you could tell there was a passage underneath. Beating your chest, you got a sympathetic boom from other corridors round about.

The little girl, growing panic-stricken, hung back, and Grundy had to coax her. "D'nise, c'mon, D'nise," he called in a sort of complacent nasal whine. There was something unreasonably irritating about it. "Why doesn't he use his own language?" muttered the old man, who had been briefed on Grundy.

In those tunnels, a sudden conspicuousness invested the sounds made by feet. Prosper wore carpet slippers. Grundy set up such a sharp fussy clacking that we all, I think, tried in the Hadean light to see whether he wore high heels. My feet made no sound except sometimes a skinny thud where the rock rose unexpectedly.

We tapped a slab that looked as if it weighed many tons but was hollow like a cardboard box. Another great chunk, used as a door, was granite brought at immense labor from some other district. Roots pierced the ceiling above us.

The passages formed rectangles, and the interiors of the rectangles were cut into pillared spaces, their floors at waist height. "Phoenicians' houses," said the old man.

Sometimes the clacking heels would mince closer behind us, then the "D'nise, c'mon, D'nise!" would drop away backward. And both had goadlike, insect-like power to provoke hatred.

"Grinding-places," said the old man. "Cupboards . . . Beds cut in the stone . . . A well . . . Graves . . . A temple. Some Indian soldier has carved his name across a painting. Italians are interned in some of these tunnels. Some woman is carving little faces of Mussolini."

I felt sure violence was coming. Trying to predict its form, I pictured Ninu making a rush at Grundy, myself sticking out my foot and tripping him, Ninu's brow bursting on the rock.

The heels clacked again behind me. Nobody was speaking just then. My back became more and more tense at Grundy's pressing close, as if he was having a race with me and I didn't want to race him. At last I was able to let him pass me. Then I took the right hand of the little girl (her father was pulling her by the left hand) and said: "Do you want to go back?"

I made us all go back.

Some days later I stood at a bus stop and there was

Grundy. He addressed me in affected English, beginning his sentences with "Eyactually . . ." He told me, "Don't get on the wrong bus, because then you won't get to the right place." My bus drew in as he spoke, and he said, "You're lucky, dem lucky." He made no sign of realizing that I had been his savior.

Our plane (though we were to go northwest) rose first over the southeastern end of Malta. Creeklike bays running into the countryside, quays at every break in the cliffs, green peninsulas crowned by elaborate buildings, boats creeping round the headlands. Then sudden shreds of cloud began to slip between us and the island like the curtains of a stage.

We got to Britain and they sent me to a school out in the country. The worst that happened there was when a crater was made in the adjoining field by an unexploded "Bread-basket," a composite bomb containing incendiary bombs and other firecrackers. A pond formed in the crater.

At the end of the term I was sent back by train to spend the vacation with Olive and Finlaw at a hotel on the Bayswater Road. A man sat opposite me and smoked cigars the whole journey. So I was sick for two weeks.

When I recovered, I thought to ask where Finlaw was.

"He'll be back later," said Olive. "I want you to sleep in the middle of the bed, between us."

I slept in the middle of the bed, Olive on one side of me, but Finlaw did not arrive to occupy the other side. I found some smudges of ink on me.

"What is it painted on your leg?" I asked.

"Oh, a map of Italy," said Olive. "The boys are going to mark our progress at each bulletin."

Though Olive was in the Navy, she couldn't tie a knot.

Finlaw used to tie her tie and now I had to do it; she tried to take it off at night without untying it.

I tried to show her that trick with a rubber band (it had just been shown to me) where it appears to be over two fingers of the clenched fist, but when you open the fist it flips to the other two fingers. She said, "Sweetie, there's no hope of *me* understanding." Then she told me that a certain wreck, a Close Support Raft, in the mud of Lymington Roads, is monument to her training. An exercise with little boats; she was Breast-Line Man, assigned to go ashore and belay a breast-line to a bollard with a round-turn-and-figure-of-eight. . . .

The next night, Olive told me to lay one of my legs between hers. She slept. Around the middle of the night, I thought I was going to lose my leg. I had the idea that what was happening to it was called "gangrene." At the speed of a leaf budding, I lifted myself away without waking Olive. I left the building.

There were some steps going down toward Kensington Gardens, a balustrade beside them. As I sat there, I looked at a very small moth which had died sitting on the stone. Its two wings sloped to the stone, and had been joined to the stone by dust. Dust, stone, and moth were the same color. It looked like a flake of the stone that had peeled up, or a tiny triangular shelter, a tent.

I spent the rest of the night gazing at it, motionless, and devising a future for myself.

I wished I had taken a few more of Olive's Bourbon biscuits before I left. Then I reflected that I did not need them, and that though I had often gone a day or two without eating I did not know the meaning of this *hunger* that people mentioned.

It must have been fourteen or fifteen or sixteen years later when I again saw Malta: the sites of the Auberge de France and the Opera House were still empty, slogans on walls said "Vote No. 1 Borg" and "Try Dom" and "Vote No. 1 Ellul Galea il Poet," there was a Caravaggio exhibition in a little museum in Valletta, they were brushing the neolithic stones of Hal Tarxien with a preserving fluid, and a windmill above Ggantija on Gozo had just had its top blown off by the wind.

I wanted to come by sea but I had to come again by air, and I found that Malta, like any toy, is made to be seen from the sky. Far off we saw Gozo, Comino, and Malta itself lying in a line toward us. We passed southward of them, inspected the southern cliffs, and turned inward. It seemed a picture rotating upon my window; if I could believe it was farther off than the glass, it was at any rate no more than a sharp shaky model constructed in fantasy for a child, though long ago, in the seventeenth century, mainly.

A seventeen-mile plank of limestone, tilted, its high Africa-ward edge supported by the great cliffs, its low Europe-ward edge invaded by drowned valleys. Sharply defined tables face each other across teeming countryside. Hundreds upon hundreds of fields no bigger than English back gardens, green and buff and, toward the eastern end, red. By almost every field a building. (And, as I knew, for almost every building above, a cave beneath.) Every farmhouse magnificent with Baroque façade. On almost every hilltop a large village which might be called a small town; compact in itself, but hardly a literal stone's throw from the next. On each villageless hill a palace, castle, or crucifix higher than the hill itself. To each village its church big enough for a cathedral; twin spires, sweating golden domes; and as if these were not enough, churches as huge at empty crossroads in the country. Several ports against every inlet from St. Paul's Bay to Marsa Xlokk, and around the drowned-valley system the towns merge, Valletta being the midpoint.

I knew the map now, and I took a course as far away from Valletta as it is possible on Malta to walk—to the Speranza Valley, the Chadwick Lakes, the Fulka Gap in the Victoria Lines, crenelated houses on Wardija Ridge; places I had not found before, but I knew the wind pumps, the old watchtowers turned into granaries, the blindfolded horses plodding round wells, the tattered Union Jack flying oddly over a patch of cactus, and the innumerable dry-stone walls that break the wind and make Malta from head height seem entirely stone. The piece of black cloth slanting over a stick might have been the same scarecrow that once scared me in the night, the dogs confined to roof-tops might have been the same that barked so furiously at me before, the disused curve of a straightened road might have been one of the waste plots I had chosen for my sleep, the fields might have been the same from which I pulled up a potato or two, the stone water channel might have been the same from which I drank, and the great scaffolds of bomb smoke might still have been standing on the cities at the farther rim of the landscape.

Between masses of cactus crowning rubble walls, a track suddenly turned over the edge of internal cliffs into a solitary valley, Wied Gnejna, descending to the western coast. Ramifications of it led to the wild bay called Fomm ir-Rih, "Wind's Mouth"; in the other direction—over the neck of a little headland incorporating a perfect rock table—to Civilian Bay, with concrete stairway from the cliff-top hotel. All this still seemed new ground. But one day from the side of the Wied tal Pwales I turned into a deep lane twisting up Qalagh Hill to a gate and pavement leading into a cave chapel. Behind the iron railing were bottles of wine, clusters of large candles hanging from nails, statues, and a shattered Italian inscription put together with cement. I recognized it: I had read it as "amnesty of a hundred days for anyone breaking the gourds." Perhaps it was an indulgence of a hundred days for anyone making pilgrimage to Lourdes. Anyway, on the strength of it I had taken the wine bottles with me to my hide-out.

It came back to me how I had asked people to explain the strange inscriptions on wayside crucifixes and statuettes in lighted niches, and had thus begun to learn Latin. "Magister Magnus Lascaris in 1651 rendered this vale fertile and enviable, which once, sterile, had envied other vales" (on the huge carved gateway of a simple field, near the town of the "Siggievi incolae"). *"Prior credidi"*—"I first believed" (motto of Naxxar, which claims it was the first town converted by St. Paul; I asked a priest, and he declined *primus* and conjugated *credo*). Mosta church "of the Virgin restored to the stars." The Porte des Bombes built *"ad majorem commoditatem populi"* (though it so incommodes the traffic, that I was too afraid of the horn blowing and collisions ever to walk through it). And country churches with rough little messages in mixed Latin-Maltese: "This chapel is *not* a chapel of refuge for criminals." (I took no notice of that.)

Finally I went where I had certainly never been before, on the ferry to Gozo. Gozitan workers returning for the weekend all seemed to know each other, and we drew into Mgarr under its fort and spire. Gozo has a hollow middle, around which stand more than a dozen table mountains, their flat tops at equal height. Each flat top is encrusted with a village—some rambling to extraordinary length, or pinched to narrow isthmuses, according to the course of the demarcating crags. These villages are crowded with inquisitive children, and wherever else you go, an interminable line of houses looks down on you from at least one of the horizons round about. For instance from what seemed a remote rough track I looked up to see Xghara on my right and Naffara on my left, Qala farther to the left (beyond Nadur, which I could not see), and Zebbug showing, though it was three valleys away.

The crags are of prickly coral, with thickets of cactus and dry grass choking their bases, and below them the slopes are terraced into tiny fields. Picking my way from field to field, or sometimes by paths where pigeons and lizards and long black snakes escaped from under my feet, I rounded a corner into one of the valleys that pass through to the coast. The citadel of Rabat, which looks down all these valleys, was behind me whenever I turned my head, and a colossus of Christ stood on one of two conical hills. Marsalforn was the name of the little town, all windows in groups of three, around the square head of the cove.

A black lane turned into a white lane, that into a smaller one, then into a path, and then into a farmyard beset with yapping dogs. The farmer's wife, who was going to visit a neighbor, showed me a way across a valley by a succession of threadlike paths along banks, through thickets, up steps. Lean and with bushy black eyebrows, she walked barefoot, like me, but unlike me she carried her heavy basket on her head.

The *rdum* are the cutaway slopes all round Gozo and the upper side of Malta. They begin abruptly with a scarp along the top, end in a chaos of boulders lying in the edge of the sea. In places the two are connected by slides of rubble. There are zones that have slumped, and small tilted blocks that have calved from the plateau like icebergs from a glacier. People have built mazes of walls and terraces. A boulder that looks as if it is merely pausing on its way down to the water is used as the base in a web of walls.

I found myself a ledge, and in return for water which I carried up from one of the five wells sunk in the gravel of a watercourse I got some food from the farm wife. Then I lay for an uncertain number of days, enclosed in a basket of flies' lines. I watched two hawks drift a thousand feet above me, or stabbed a patch of sand and listened to its multiple sibilance. In view was a red beach. It was supposed to be Calypso's cove, where Odysseus was washed ashore. On top of the hill was Calypso's cave, where Odysseus lay in torpor nine years.

Nothing that I remember occurred to me except a phrase: "the sea spectator of the land." As I stared blankly in front of me, a snake, tied in a thumbknot, took itself past my feet.

. . . I ate acorns, chestnuts, sow thistles,
honeysuckles, snow, snakes and lizards,
frog spawn, grubs, clay, laundry starch . . .

. . . when I first got pastels, I thought
they were only what pavement-artists use.
I drew on the Oxford sidewalk a nude
like Goya's Maja and began a sky seen
through prison bars (I was going to title it
"Transcendence") but by then I had worn
down my Moss Green, Brick, and Caput
Mortuum Deep . . .

. . . Didikoys in the New Forest stole my
tent and showed me how to make a "bender"
instead: withies stuck in the grass verge of
the road and bent over so their tops stick in
the hedge, a tarpaulin laid across them . . .

. . . begged ice creams from vendors,
drew pictures, told stories, sang, taught
languages, wrote letters for Gypsies, looked
after children, took messages, carried parcels
across borders, collected hens' eggs from
hedgerows, caught jarfuls of the Great Red
Sedge-Fly for fishermen, gathered gritty
horsetails for housewives to scour pots with,
took the cream off milk bottles on doorsteps,
got apple cores and ends of bread out of
trash cans, made friends, worked, found
money . . .

. . . a lane coming out of foothills made a
gallery low above the road it was about to
join. There were two woodmen's cottages built
into the bank, and I stepped onto their roof
and slept there, the nest of tiles between the
chimneys being warm . . .

. . . through a night I watched
mushrooms come up . . .

some miles

I came from Youlgreave and Lathkill Dale, and where my lane descended to the main Bakewell-Buxton road there was a row of tall sad houses. Rain had just ended, children—red-haired, bespectacled—were pouring out to play in one of the front gardens. With them around me, I went up to the open front door, and their mother appeared at an upstairs landing and called down to me. She was nursing a baby—a neighbor's baby that had been left with her, I thought she said.

They sat me down at the kitchen table and gave me a cup of tea and a slice of Madeira cake. I was distinctly crowded, and Slike (the dog) was licking my feet and Quinth (the cat) was trying to get on my lap. I opened my folder of samples, and we turned through every one, and at every one they said: "Oh! That's . . . good."

Then the children showed me their pictures. One child showed me a sea colored by numbers. Another showed me a papier-mâché elephant. Another showed me a book about outer space, which he got as second prize for art.

Then the mother—who was also red-haired and bespectacled, but very large—found yesterday's evening paper and showed me something about a lady who lives in the West Indies and paints. There was a photograph of one of her pictures, which was priced at a hundred pounds. I said that was because it took at least forty hours to paint; but I was going to make one just as good in half an hour, or perhaps three quarters, and I was going to ask only for a meal, if she could give me one, and perhaps a bit extra if the picture seemed worth it. I said that was called undercutting. I said I wouldn't take more than one pound if she offered it. She said, "You see, I don't know that we can afford even that kind of money. People get the wrong idea because this house is so big, but actually we're bankrupt.

"Still," she said, "I was wishing I could get Treeza's portrait done, only yesterday when I saw this bit in the paper. I suppose you couldn't wait till my husband comes home?" I said I hadn't had anything to eat and thus preferred to push on and try somewhere else. I said I would have done Treeza for love, otherwise. "Will you be coming here again?" asked Treeza, aged five, the only one without spectacles, and with a sulky look. I said perhaps I would when she was older.

"Do you have a mum and dad?" Treeza asked.

"No."

"So you're adopted?"

"Sort of," I said.

"So you used to be a girl, when you were born?"

"That's not what adopted means," said her mother.

"But the baby's name is Michael, and she's adopted."

"Oh dear," said the mother to me, "I don't know why those people did such a silly thing as call a girl Michael." The baby was now asleep in her arms. "I'll never stop having to try and explain it to these kids."

Probably the baby was named Michal after the daughter of Saul who looked on King David dancing and "despised him in her heart."

At the front door the woman, pointing across the river to Ashford village, told me I might try Mrs. Brassmith

with the art shop, or old Colonel Fulchatt, the archaeologist, halfway out along the road to Headstones Edge.

"Can I mention your name?" I asked.

"Oh, he won't remember me; he's over eighty and lives
in the past."

In front of the bridge a gentleman in a velvet jacket
had just finished a drawing in sepia ink. He was cleaning
it with an eraser. I asked to have a look, since I too was
an artist. It showed the trees rising among the houses
across the river.

"What beautiful straight lines," I said.

This made the gentleman defensive. "I don't use any
ruler. Shall I show you how I draw a straight line?" He
held the pen still with one hand, and pulled the paper
away with the other.

He had a patent collapsible easel and a patent collapsible stool, and as he folded them up he asked what I sat
on when I drew. I was surprised, and then answered that
I sit on the ground, or stand up, or perhaps I lean against
a hedge.

"A hedge?" he said. "How can one lean against a
hedge?" Then he asked if I had any training. I thought
he must mean some kind of yoga. "You just have to
spread your weight," I said. He turned abruptly back to
his eraser.

Mrs. Brassmith was away on the Continent buying
objets d'art. After asking my way at the post office, I left
the village by a lane that went rolling gradually upward
to four cottages and Colonel Fulchatt's property beyond
them.

I failed to find the front door and was wandering on the
back lawn when the colonel's wife saw me and asked me

if I had come about the insurance. Either she had dim eyes or insurance men dress informally in the purlieus of the Derbyshire Wye.

I said I had come at the recommendation of a Mrs. Vastlegg. (As the woman had declined to tell me her name, I paid her out by inventing one.) "Mrs. Vastlegg? I must have met her at some village do," said the colonel's wife. "We hardly ever go into the village nowadays."

She ushered me into a large room and took a dust cover off a settee so I could sit down. Then (first saying, with a shy laugh, "I'm sorry about that screen over the fireplace, but if we don't put it there the jackdaws come in!") she went to apprise her husband.

I was summoned into the kitchen. Its yellow limestone was full of the warmth of the fire, and intimate possessions crowded the walls and corners.

I showed the old colonel a portrait of someone about his own age. "This is an archaeologist called Alan Rowe," I said. "Do you know him?"

"No."

"Well, anyhow," I said, "when I showed this to Mrs. Vastlegg she mentioned that you are the archaeologist of the district. And she told me you found a village on stilts under the village green here, and brought Pitt-Rivers to see it."

"Pitt-Rivers!" the colonel exclaimed. "I'm old, but not as old as that. He was before even my time. He did come here once. I did find the postholes of one pile dwelling, but it was some way up the river. I daren't mention anything in the village any more. If I find a five-foot skeleton it ends up seven foot at the least—ancient men about here all got to be giants, you know. . . . And what's that?"

I had accidentally exposed a caricature.

"I have no intention," said the colonel, "of leaving my grandchildren (who've all cleared out by now, and good riddance) that kind of picture of the old buffer for them to laugh at."

"But what about these skeletons you dig up?" I asked impudently. "Don't you think they're unhappy too, about being looked at in their latter state?"

"Oh, but I think skeletons are beautiful! Much more so than live bodies. Why, you should see a little girl I've got out in my shed just now! My wife gets jealous of my skeletons; she won't have them in the house at night. . . .

"At a site called Bambata in Rhodesia," he reminisced, "Armstrong and I worked twenty-five feet straight down in soft white wood ash. If anyone had come near and stepped on it, phooph! we'd have been smothered, dead, under it all. We just had one Matabele servant who walked out along a tree trunk to pull our buckets up. We had to camp eleven miles away, at the only spot where there were a few drops of water, and walk in every day. . . . I was Abbé Breuil's chauffeur while he was in Britain. It was an education to listen to him, though he was asleep most of the time—he just woke up by instinct if we passed a black cat or a clergyman; then he'd try to seize the wheel and run them over. . . . I have a knack for sensing burials, even in deep snow. . . . The other day, in thirty-seven, we found a mammoth's tooth in the patch of glacial clay down in this garden. . . . Six-year-olds miss nothing. My grandson picked a microscopic thing out and it proved to be a bone from the inside of a haddock's ear. . . . Armstrong found a fish scale. My wife laughed and nearly blew it away. She asked whether it was worth digging all that earth away to find it—he was quite offended. . . . The duke's servant spilt grain on the bones.

. . . I can never publish anything. It costs three hundred pounds for a proper article with illustrations. But Stuart Piggott's my friend and he slips articles in 'with acknowledgements to Colonel E. Fulchatt for letting me use his notes.' I don't get any fame. But what would I do with it if I had it? . . . It has been shown that in the Upper Paleolithic the maximum population of Britain was two hundred souls. . . . What I'm working on now is a Megalithic missionary who came to our valley, but seems to have landed among a pocket of Paleolithic survivals, not Neoliths, like all around. You can tell because at the same period they use chert one side of the river and flint the other. Now this missionary came from Andalucia or the Cyclades, traveling probably in great pomp. He had his tomb built to his own specifications. But when he was dead they did the dirty on him, the Paleoliths: they made it a magnificent long barrow on the outside, but inside it's quite mean. The nettles will be over it again since I last got down there. I can only manage two or three visits a year. You should see the way the Peak country sprouts water in the winter. . . ."

Thus the talk dwelt on archaeology till the colonel was in a compliant temper. He was no less stubborn about not having his own portrait made, but he said, "I'll clear out of the way while he draws you, my dear, if you think you're worth drawing." His wife modestly didn't know whether to say yes or no, and I began to get my pastels out as if the matter was already decided.

I would rather have drawn the old gentleman's face, an ancient nut deeply matured for the manipulation of light. Mrs. Fulchatt's main feature was her very wide amiable smile. I asked her to choose an object to keep her eyes fixed on. She said, "Would you go and open a wall cupboard in the corner? Then I'll be able to look at my china." Toward the end I realized that the paper I had used was too light in tint to let me render her white hair effectively. She said, "I'll never live this down!" I felt unreasonably hurt. She searched for a pound to give me, but couldn't find one and said it would have to wait till her husband came in. She told me to take a sherry out in the garden while waiting for a supper of scrambled eggs. I found the colonel digging potatoes. The gnats gathered round my ankles while I stood and listened to yet more stories of archaeology and of past wars.

I was given a toasting fork and I knelt before the hearth toasting. Then we sat at the table. I mistook the salt and pepper for a pair of binoculars. Not till darkness had almost filled the old kitchen did they ask me to pull the light cord. I stood up and pulled a long cobweb by mistake. The colonel looked suspicious of my eyesight.

"You relive in yourself," he told me, "the tides of Normans, Danes, Angles, Romans, Belgae, Brythons, Goidels, Urnfield Folk, Beaker Folk, across this island. . . . The recurrence of nomadic persons in a society which has long passed their stage is explained by atavism: from each crude stage a component, steadily dwindling, survives in human nature, and soaks out in a proportionate number of individuals in each age. . . ."

His wife and I were still waiting with trepidation for his verdict on the picture. He quite liked it. We were relieved. Now no doubt it is dusty in some cupboard and saddens them a little when they happen to move something that is in front of it. "We ought to have framed it really. . . . But—well—it's a pity it had to be my declining years. . . . That young fellow who came here and drew it, I wonder where he is now?"

On the kitchen wall hung a silver dish embossed with a swell-bellied nymph who played a kind of lute; underneath, the word CIGALE.

"Are you a classicist?" the colonel asked. "Can you tell me about the legend of Cybele?"

Confused by his misreading of it, I thought perhaps Cigale was the nymph who got turned into a cicada but went on making music. Or was there some Spanish word for cigars or Gypsies at the bottom of it? Yet I had been eating fried *cigales* only a week or two before.

"Where did you get the dish?" I asked the colonel.

"From a dealer in a town in Picardy. Every day he was reducing his prices, because the Germans were getting nearer and nearer, and every day I went and bought another treasure. Finally I bought this, and then next day the Germans got there—shop and dealer were no more. . . .

"I was in charge of chemical operations. Once I was ordered to clear Ypres high street for transport. It was full of the debris of the houses. I had to have it all blown aside with explosives. But that blew the surface of the street away, and the surface turned out to be just a skin over a line of cellars. In every one of those cellars I found a candle and a few fine objects. Each cellar was the treasury of a house, bricked off, but a candle in place for the day it might have to be opened up. Well, there was no time to spare, I had to blow all the rubble back into the cellars to make the road level again. All those clocks and medallions and charms must still be there under Ypres high street. . . .

"I was always working with our side's gas, as well as being a target for the other side's, so in the end they had to send me home, and I've had to stay up in these hills ever since. I've got a hip joint made of an acrylic compound too. . . ." Then he told many stories of rough sleeping places, in saps full of water, Flanders woods, mined and booby-trapped villages, tin-roofed huts on which hail and shrapnel were falling.

Meanwhile, sleepy in front of the fire, I was troubled by slight drafts which the old people didn't even notice. They led me round the cold outer provinces of the house to show me some pictures and ornaments. I proved to have no expert knowledge of them. They showed me a solid chert fireplace directly under a window. It seemed impossible, but by a sleight of stonework the chimney twisted away into the wall to one side. They unbolted and unchained the front door to show me the archway, in which a former owner had carved imitation Norman moldings.

"I feel dreadful about having to lock you outside for the night," said Mrs. Fulchatt. "It's a terrible rough lawn, I'm afraid. I do hope the wind doesn't blow too cold. Perhaps you would be more sheltered between the sheds there?"

"My dear, he's weatherproof!" said the colonel.

I did not feel weatherproof. I politely said I believed the colonel was more weatherproof than I.

"Well, we are all weatherproof, to tell the truth," said the colonel. "Skin is weatherproof. Remarkable substance. Waterproof—almost the only substance that is. Readily washable, perfectly fitting, self-repairing . . . But not as beautiful as the bare bones."

And, while we stood there in the doorway, which was draftier than the garden, the old man rolled his sleeve up to show me how the hair lies down the upper arm but across the forearm, so that the rain would run off when we or our ape ancestor squatted out in it, arms folded across our chests.

The lawn was so fine that I hesitated to stick my skewers into it. I slung the tent between two ancient apple trees, tying the guy ropes to them, instead of using the tent poles. At intervals in the night stillborn fruit came ripping down through the leaves. A coconut hung on a string, and I woke to the rapping on it of chaffinches. I was rolling my tent up when the colonel called me in for breakfast.

"Skeletons didn't get out of their shed in the night, did they?" he asked me. And he gave me an anatomical atlas—*Trans-Visions of Anatomical Chromographs*—to improve my drawing. He said, "I have another little one for bones only, which is all I need."

We walked together to the gate. "Quite honestly," said the old lady, giggling and overjutting her chin the way people do when they are afraid what they say may be stamped on—"quite *honestlayer,* what I enjoy is hearing the King's English for once!" And she gave an imitation of the bad grammar of the locals. Of course I had taken color from them while I was with them. That is how I get my education.

"Call on us if you ever pass this way again," said the old man. "If we're still alive. But what I hope is that in the end I shall crash the car and kill us both together."

The lane outside (the colonel had told me) was a deep dusty rut when they first came to live there. Edward I once rode along it. (I seem to see Colonel Fulchatt at his garden gate to watch the cavalcade, holding perhaps his tame mammoth on a short leash.) Repeatedly coated with tarmac, the lane has risen and widened between its sloping banks till now it is level with the cornfields. Thus an archaeologist sees even roads as layers rather than ribbons. A mile or so beyond, the road rises to that point which is called Longstone, Headstones Edge, or Monsal Head.

The ground gapes; two gorges meeting at a sharp angle are Monsal Dale and Miller's Dale. Along the floor of both flows an upper part of the same river I had crossed back in the village. Everything was yet more profound in the morning mist. While I looked from the brink, a train shot out of a tunnel underneath me.

A footpath plunged to the left between tree tops into Monsal Dale, but, looking as if someone had cut it with a spade, it was narrower than the wheels of my basket. So I went down the road slanting the other way into Miller's Dale. My feet flopped unequally on the steep asphalt. Cows hugged the slope beside me. The wide bowl of the valley bottom was dotted with ragwort. The river poured along in pools on the grass. There was no traffic; the crisping of a weed in the current could entertain the whole valley with sound. The sun warmed the mist away. A broken notice in a hedge said, seeming to legalize my well-being:

PROPERTY

WILL BE PROSECUTED.

By Order.

A mile of valley. Then the road is pushed away from the river by a mill, and uses the flank of a brief tributary valley to regain height. At the foot of this ascent it also forks, and the place looks like the foot of stairs in a house. I sit on a strip of grass to draw. I wonder why the wind is now so noisy; I find it is a weir behind the mill wall. Starting forward again, I find the road splits not into two but into three; they braid the slope, and all rejoin at the top. I don't know which to take; all look indispensable. I am in danger of coming to a standstill among these details— yet it is a danger which is in every half-mile of scenery. I would wish to make clear the relations of these things in space; they are not like points along flat lines on a map, but like landings and cupboards and windows in a house. Description reveals only the need for a diagram; a diagram, with a few leaves added, becomes one of my roadscapes. The road builders themselves, with their dotted white lines, draw a diagram to point up what they have made.

I took the steepest way, walking backward and pulling my basket at my toes. The three roads rejoined at the top just past a village. Now the road was a gallery along the top of cliffs, overlooking a wilder part of Miller's Dale. A few cars used the road. The people in them were too low-slung even to know they were passing a view over the most magnificent rock bastions in England, grouped shadowily about the windings of a green river. And if those on the offside catch sight of something, those on the onside are too lethargic to crane their necks. Where the road swung away into the tableland, a track kept to the valley and aimed past some more mills. I opened the gate and tested the surface of the track. It would shake my boxes of pastels too much. I got back on the road and followed it round a corner onto the upland. The only trees were protective wings stooping over homesteads. In such bleak country the road-worshipper faces his road in its simplicity, its familiar white line swarms straight from the sky to his feet.

. . . "Here, this will be more use to you than
us—you can measure your mileage with it."
Little instrument with dial and toothed
wheel. I didn't say so, but it was for running
along roads on maps, not real ones . . .

. . . when streams and the sea were too cold
to bathe in, I got an underarm spray so I
wouldn't smell too bad in houses . . .

droudionnades

Replies I gave to the question "What's your name?" in
the one month of August 1954:

> Hellenger
>
> Hastrel
>
> Traluce
>
> Gly
>
> Commolane
>
> Hontiphas
>
> Calerno
>
> Droudionnades

> Slang Song
>
> O Holy Limb
>
> Trumpet Upon the Mekong
>
> Tinder Chasm Hymn
>
> Verses and titles of verses
> Wandered at brain's gates
> But under virgins' curses
> Some never met their mates.
>
> Spain and Portugal Tango
>
> Egypt and China Pavane . . .

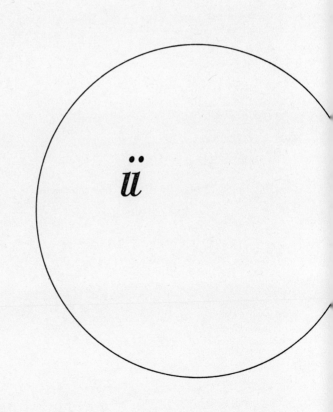

. . . when I was a child it took me about two hours to get to sleep. I would lie against a tree with a root cutting into my neck. I thought this might help to disconnect the brain . . .

. . . for use of their gardens as my bedrooms, I have to thank the Galleon Hotel in Burgh Heath, the Ministry of Supply in Chessington, the Central Milk Distribution Board in Thames Ditton, the Master of St. John's College in Oxford, Derry & Tom's store (roof garden) in London, and private citizens too numerous to name . . .

. . . writing a poem at night with my head out of the tent. Lights from a distant road, I could see where I was writing but not what. Left the inkpot outside. Woke and reached out to write another line—stubbed the nib on ice . . .

I hitched a driver who was going my way.
At Alconbury on the A 1 highway
He stopped to have a smoke. Then in a sly way

He had another. Dusk now filled the sky and
I shammed asleep. He breathed a hasty sigh and
Applied the clutch—applied it to my thigh and . . .

. . . GRIT FOR ROADS, a sign that made me
smile. Those little piles of grit can be
most comfortable . . .

. . . pastel outdoors: wind disposes of loose
powder, keeps the fingers unsweaty for
rubbing, but makes the paper flap. I had an
old garter to hold it to a board, but the elastic
was weak. Once sitting by a pond, I dipped my
only Sunproof Orange in it, thinking I was
using watercolor . . .

. . . had me draw a new litter of puppies at
an inn . . .

. . . had me paint a new house name on the
gate. Explained that a condition of sale was
that the old name not be kept. The old name
was "Camrhos" . . .

. . . had me draw a black shiny dog—
birthday card for a little girl asleep upstairs.
I used scraper board. The father had to amuse
the dog with a ball, holding it in the dog's
mouth as long as possible while I drew. The
overworked ball split into crumbs . . .

. . . paid me to collect graffiti, folklore,
jokes, and dialogue, and report back in a
month . . .

soppy date

I was probably about ten and Betty Tanner thirteen.
People said she was a dreadful girl. I met her on a path
of white-grey sand running at the edge of a strip of trees
called the Warden's Belt.

We walked along. I mentioned innocently how I'd discovered that if you lie on your front with your hands
under you, after a time you could get a nice feeling. "Do
you find that?"

"Yes," she said.

We came to a green of the golf course, where a sprinkler
was going round and round. We started to run at it. I dug
my heels in and stopped at the last moment; Betty Tanner
ran on through and got wetter than she intended.

Her dress and hair wept on her. "I'll have to take my
dress off and let it dry," she said. We found a clearing
in the gorse bushes. I was to stand guard.

I stood guard patiently and didn't peep, till she called
me with a loud "Cm'ere!"

"Yes?" I said. There was a pause.

"You're a soppy date," said Betty Tanner.

(It was the vogue expression then. I conceived an antique name: *Sopydates*. A monarch. Oriental. Persian.
Sopu-data.)

"Why?" I asked.

She shivered and stumbled, putting her dress back on.
It was no drier, for there was no sun.

We came through the gaps in the gorse to the path. She

turned back along it the way we had come. So I turned that way. So she turned the other way. I climbed a tree.

Sopu-data, the Sun-Given, became King Senandates the Thirty-first. He became Sunacherar. Sunacherar became a land. Its language was Cherart . . .

. . . when Derwentwater was frozen over, the children of Borrowdale used to skate over to school in Keswick . . .

. . . had me help with a map the children were making of a neighboring common, with the roads around it. I drew lines freehand, made dirty thumb marks. Father impatiently took the pencil, ruled straight lines to a corner, meticulously laid the ruler across the corner while erasing the parts of the line beyond it . . .

. . . I bought a bottle of banana yogurt, mixed some in milk, and stood them in warm water all night, getting up every so often to reheat it. I expected all the milk to turn to yogurt—banana yogurt . . .

. . . they took me to meet the secretary of the Society of Watercolorists, and he had me stay to tea. Asked me: "What are the most beautiful things?" He had to ask me twice. I suggested, "Roads. Clouds." "I would add thighs," he said. "The underside of a boy's thigh." Later he told me he wished he were the saddle of a boy's bicycle . . .

. . . huge neglected house for sale on the outskirts of Banstead. Garden a shambles, broad sweep of trees giving way to piles of rubble and crumbling flights of steps. The house was divided in two, each part had seven bedrooms. I determined to sleep in them all, thus passing a fortnight . . .

. . . once I had a watch. It gained an hour a day and I put it forward five on Sundays. Would have let it stop, but it was the kind that winds as you move. I kept it because it was nice to be asked the time and give provoking answers . . .

. . . took me out to "advise on artistic aspects" of his garden. He gave me a hammer and some copper nails, and told me to wriggle under the fence and drive the nails in a ring round the base of a beech in his neighbor's grounds. "Its drip is killing everything in my border. I tried injecting it with nitric acid, that didn't kill it and I'm told this will. Don't make a noise—close the bark over the nails." I pushed the nails in with clinging blows, closing the bark like Eglon's belly over the dagger . . .

. . . I rescued a bullfinch from the mouth of a cairn terrier. It seemed unhurt, and before letting it go I drew its portrait. The same afternoon I saw a hawk fly over, chased by a squadron of little birds—among them a bullfinch that I believed I knew . . .

. . . came on some people looking for their car key, which they had lost while walking by a canal; joined the search, found the key. They offered me a bed for the night, but changed their mind because "we haven't got one six and a half feet long." It needn't be six and a half feet long, but it needs to be without endboards. I stick my feet over the end, and for once they are free of pressure. On the ground this is not possible except at the top of a cliff . . .

. . . took no notice of the signs on old houses being demolished or remodeled, "Keep Out— Falling Masonry," till one night I woke with a brick pirouetting beside my head . . .

. . . another use for the sea: if you go swimming when you have a cold, salt water gets in your nose and clears it . . .

. . . wasp bite—hand swollen up to the middle of the palm, elbow and shoulder hurting too. I made myself a sling, and then some people gave me a poultice of Anti-Phlogiston and told me to change it three times a day. I waited till I was well away from the house and then I turned and muttered: "How can I?" . . .

roseland

My guardians took me on a trip to Cornwall. We stayed in a guesthouse at Gerrans, on the Roseland peninsula. They were put in a bedroom upstairs, but I was put in a small extension at the side of the house, with a door of its own. The landlord said, "So the young man can come in any time he likes, ha ha!" My guardians were uneasy.

We walked down to Portscatho, the harbor village just below Gerrans. A brass band was playing, and crowds of holidaymakers like ourselves gathered. The band took an interval, was reassembled with some difficulty from the pubs, and struck up the "Cornish Floral Dance." Everyone followed the band, dancing, or at any rate skipping, up to a square at the end of the village, and then danced round and round. We danced past the doors of a dance hall, and saw only two pairs inside. We could still hear the distant bellow of "Fiddle, cello, big bass drum, / Cornet, flute and euphoni-um" when we went to bed in the other village.

I forgot to make any use of my separate door. On the last day of our stay, we were bathing and lying on the beach, and I dressed and slipped away. I wandered round Portscatho by myself. At the end of the village I came to a stile into the fields, and a girl was getting over it. She wore shorts, and I glimpsed the springing of one buttock. I asked her to meet me there at half past nine in the evening. She laughed and said, "You bet!"

Then I went back and stood waiting for my elders at

the head of a ramp that led down onto the beach. I hadn't thought of making another pickup. I saw on the concrete what I at first took for a wet brown rubber mat; it was a large fish. A tough-looking teen-ager, with a hat that said just "Welcome," called out to a man in a swimsuit, "Did you catch it?" "Shot it, actually," he replied. "We were doing some bottom-surveying in the bay." "Sounds dirty!" she remarked to me. Such words didn't have the same effect as the glimpse, but after trying to be witty with her for a few minutes I said, "Meet me here at half past ten?" She said, "Bit late, isn't it? You ought to be in bed by then."

Then I thought I might as well spread my net as wide as possible, so I walked around some more, and I found a girl rowing a boat in and tying it up. I asked her to meet me at that very place at ten o'clock. She said she would think about it.

That evening the elders took deck chairs out onto the front lawn and sat there listening to the crickets. But the plot of ground next door was empty except for a half-built house, so I climbed over the fence and got out that way. I went by a path down through the fields to the stile. Amazingly enough, the first girl was there. It must have been the last night of her holiday too. She was called Rita Langham and told me that she was half Belgian. I caught her pretending to pronounce things un-Englishly. We spent some time arguing in a dark lane under trees. I said I wouldn't kiss her any more except in bed. I got rid of her, or she of me, and having missed the ten o'clock tryst I hurried for the half-past-ten one, but got confused and waited in the place for the ten o'clock one. Or perhaps I did it deliberately, so as to be able to tell myself why no one came, and to assure myself that while I was waiting in one place the third girl (whom I had spoken to second) was waiting in River Street just out of sight. When I got back to my room I found that the elders had been nosing in it and had left a note: "Come and say good night to us when you come back." Since it was so late, I didn't. But then my foster father appeared outside the window and said, "Your mother's gone all skittish and wants to play some games on our last night." He was pretending not to be suspicious, but I lifted the bedclothes with my knees and hands so as to make it look as if I was hiding someone else, and he struck a match and looked in more carefully.

Something (perhaps a degree's difference in the angle of the cheek, or a millimeter off the length of the lip, or perhaps a syllable spoken in a certain tune) kept Rita Langham in my mind and brought me back years later to the forest rampart of Devonshire and the crossing of the Tamar.

Mist flowed up from the sea and left only the lanes, deep between their banks, as clear tunnels under it. Near Liskeard a middle-sized black dog, with a boil between his toes, fell in with me and would not stop following. We passed down a complex of lanes which brought us to a tiny old one-roomed building with a stone roof, placed over a stream. It was called the Dupath Well Chapel. Water from a holy spring passed through a shallow basin the length of a man, so that people could lie down in it to be cured of their ailments. The dog lay in the cool water, and I left him there. Out in the sea from the cliffs by Tintagel I saw the tips of what must have been a giant seaweed, floating to the surface over an area of several hundred feet. Then through the inland where the slag heaps rise from china-clay quarries, some still shining white cones, others fluted by erosion and merged into a new landscape by vegetation; down to Roseland. The road repeatedly loops inland to a village which the pirates in the old days could not see, then down again to a landfall— Hemmick, Caerhays, Portholland, Portloe, Pendower, Porthbean, Porthcurnick, Portscatho. Between, the path runs at the foot of a down-curving field, and below it is first a band of scrub, then an earthen cliff, then grass and stagnant pools of spray lying among the top ends of the rock, then the rock strata themselves, always sloping up onto the land, like several layers of iron paint applied to the slope; difficult to erode, they yield only undulating or dimpled shapes. Below them again comes a rough rocky floor, then sand under shallow water with breakers racing over it. Finding places to sleep was strangely difficult. I came to a long beach, or series of bays, part shingly, part rocky, part sandy, between curtains of rock. There was almost no sea breeze, or even waves, at this season. I swam so much every day that I had wave drunkenness, and all evening I would feel as if still in the pull of swinging water.

Beyond Portscatho I walked along the path with a girl and her dog. The way passed through a cave; the girl would not, the dog could not, go through, and they turned back. I came to the three features collectively called St. Anthony in Roseland: village (Bohortha) on the hilltop; lighthouse and other buildings on the tip (Zone Point); church, manor, and Nissen huts on a lawn (Place) by the edge of a water (Porthcuel or Porthcuil or Percuil or Portcuil or Purcuil, the last two on the same signpost). And the church of St. Just-in-Roseland (or Ecclesia Sancti Justi de Lansioch in Ros—or church of St. Jestyn of

Lanzeague in the Headland). And St. Mawes, where the clergyman told me visitors often come with notebooks to copy the "legends" on the tombstones. I went and looked, but they were Biblical quotations, not stories. I hired a rowboat for an hour, and rowed into a side creek to view and paint the church from the water, and to see if I could perhaps devise a legend about it. The church stood among pine trees; the graveyard behind it rose to a ridge, full of bright foliage and blossoms. There were curlews, sand-pipers, little bitterns. I stayed too long, devising my legend, and the ebbing tide exposed a bar and stranded me in the inlet. I could have gone on with my painting, but conditions had changed and blades of mist were sliding in along the sides of the creek. I wondered whether to forfeit my deposit on the boat and join the water-borne world of the old Celtic saints, who used to sail from peninsula to peninsula on tombstones.

I sat on some grass in front of St. Mawes Castle, look-ing at the waterway, called Carrick Roads, which was filled with mist; but I hadn't noticed that the mist was receding, till suddenly and awesomely the silhouette of Pendennis Castle on the other side appeared above, with another bright bank of mist behind it. The passenger ferry from St. Mawes to Falmouth was steered on that occasion by a novice steersman. Maneuvering out through a crowd of little boats, it rocked and bumped several, and then took the wind from a yacht. The irate yachtsman raised what looked like an arquebus, and almost all the pas-sengers fled from the rail of the ferry, except me and an elderly couple. "Why didn't you run away?" said the old man, who was of military bearing. "Too lazy," I said, trying to make it look as if I really meant "Too dig-nified." I asked him why he and his wife hadn't run away, and he said he thought they made a poor target. Then we discussed whether the thing the yachtsman had was a harpoon gun. Then they asked me about myself, and I tried to give a satisfactory answer. Then the gentleman said, "Look here, my name is Magnus Jackson. I'll set you up in a proper studio, if you wish it."

In Gorran (or St. Goran) I had seen a monumental sculptor on one side of the street and a woodcarver on the other. In St. Mawes I had visited the studio of an artist called Molly Forestier-Walker, who showed me her publicity files and a portrait that was reproduced in the *Tatler*. I was not so much envious as sure that other people wasted their chances. I was free, but not to let my mind dwell on ideas that might need time and resources. Sometimes I pictured signs I might put up over my door: "Jecon Gregory, Skin Painter" or "Painter of Foreign Parts."

Mr. Jackson asked me what I would do if I had a studio. I said first I would give an exhibition; nothing for sale, but a notice saying that commissions would be accepted. I would charge only by time spent. Only a pound an hour. And most portraits I would finish in an hour. That would undercut the market, to say the least, since the usual thing was to charge twenty guineas for each of twenty three-hour sittings and come up with a portrait no different from mine. Mr. Jackson looked disappointed. But perhaps he told himself he could not expect philosophies from a beggar whose first concern was always his next mouthful of crumbs.

The M. V. *Newroseland* entered the wall of mist, foghorns sounding round about, and the passengers shrilly sure our steersman would hit something. We could smell Falmouth in front though we could not see it. Because the tide was low, we had to go ashore in a boat that had been detached from a buoy and taken in tow for the purpose. It happened that I was put in the first boatload, and the benevolent couple had to wait for the second. When I stepped onto the quay, I went on walking, because it seemed undignified to stand and wait for them. I may say that I have, I hope, outgrown this particular form of vanity, which is not a characteristic favoring survival.

At St. Michael's Mount it was a special day for visiting in aid of the Red Cross. I tried to walk back along the causeway as the tide was covering it, but twisted my ankle between the rocks. Near Marazion a house burned, and I drew with my pastels a brighter picture than I had ever managed before (usually my style is drab). I offered it to the owner of the house, but without success; I offered it then to the firemen, but they wouldn't buy it either. I came to Land's End, and looked down the rectangular rocks; at their bases, huge volumes of submerging foam. But because it was Land's End, litter and glass were scattered right down the cliffs.

I turned into the Porthcurno district because there are in it three Logan Stones, and I had once been fond of someone called Logan, and wondered what it meant. It means "rocking stone," and the greatest one is a slab pointing up from the end of a tremendous headland of split and battered rock. It can be moved with the finger, and once a reckless Navy officer who toppled it had to bankrupt himself having it raised again, since it was the livelihood of the village of Treen. This Logan Stone dominates a beach which stretches west from it in a single arc a mile long to Porthcurno. The dry sand was utterly smooth pure yellow. Where covered it lit the water with chrysoprase.

A path down the rocks passed the Minack Cliff Theatre.

It was just over the brink of the cliff, just round a corner from Porthcurno Bay, but the Logan Stone was visible at the edge of a great expanse of sea. There was to be a performance, and I waited for it, sleeping away the cold dull afternoon in a hollow of the rocks. Seats in the theater were rough terraces of grass shored up with stone, or comfortable impressions made in the turf. The stage was a grass semicircle, and at the back of it, seemingly on the edge of a gulf, rose some abstract all-purpose scenery—a balustrade and gate and steps and table, cut in granite blocks with simple incised decoration. A path led through the rocks to a hollow with tents, which were the dressing rooms.

At the start of the performance it was daylight, and I could see fishermen on the rocks below. Actors had to run offstage along dark rocky glens. King Arthur fought a knight on a flat projecting rock and forced him to leap off apparently into the abyss (screams from the audience). Merlin appeared in a pointed Gothic arch on the sky line behind us. Afterward I wandered into the dressing-hollow by mistake and met Guinevere taking her cloak off. She said, "Damn, I had the thing on inside out."

"Rita!" I said.

But she wasn't Rita. We are grains of sand continually shaken in a sieve.

The audience was shuffling out up the hillside, and to help them the spotlights were pointed our way, but they only dazzled our heads and left our feet in darkness. I stubbed my foot on a rock, splitting the toenail and falling against somebody.

. . . crossing a side street at night, I glanced
along it and got an eyeful of car headlights;
the next moment I met a man walking,
believed he was someone I should know, but
the dazzle on my pupil obliterated the middle
of his face.

And once across Watling Street I saw a child
I had played with when I was a child. I
hurried over to speak to him. He had entered a
phone kiosk. I stood outside, smiling at
him. He saw me, he looked alarmed, he stayed
inside. I had to go away . . .

. . . helped excavate part of Chedworth villa,
a Roman hunting box beside a lanelike
water meadow through Cotswold woods full
of pheasants, rabbits, and yellowhammers. It
was discovered a century before when a
ferret had to be dug out of a foxhole. With mice
jumping over our fingers, we opened the
north wing and found dye and fuller's
earth . . .

. . . between Hungerford and Bedwyn I
went into a barn to sleep. An old bull followed
me, butting along a heavy metal drum with
which he blocked the door. Next morning he
was in position. I looked fixedly at him and
(reaching across his barricade) patted
his head, as I had seen farm hands do. He
walked away . . .

. . . widow who wouldn't open her door and
let me in, but wanted me to see every room
of her cottage and how she had painted it. I
had to go from window to window through
the hollyhocks, while she took an inside
route to meet me . . .

. . . imagine what an inturned eyelash means
to a person who has no mirror. I rinsed
it in a stream—no good. Endured till I should
meet a girl; she would bend her face close to
mine. I met one. She was too stupid.
She couldn't understand how an eyelash can
be interned . . .

wells

At Wells I had a meal in the Swan Hotel opposite the cathedral. I went out of the dining room the wrong way and along a passage leading to the garages. It passed the kitchen, and I saw some girls looking out at me. I walked back thinking I could speak to them, but I couldn't, so I walked past yet again and threw a note in at a window to where a girl was working. The note said, "Will you please meet me here at 10 o'clock tonight?" and for all I know it fell in the stew.

I went into Wells Cathedral. I gazed at the famous inverted arches, which coil in switchback flow around the transept crossing like pythons knotting the tower together; and at the flight of contours, rather than steps, leading to the chapter house; and at the effigy of a gaunt corpse beneath the tomb of Bishop Beckington or Bekynton, looking just like me sun-bathing on rocks; and at the marvelous white cleanness of the ancient building, which a perambulating clergyman told me is because Doulting stone all the time slowly pulverizes at the surface; and at the chiming of the hour by the clock in the north wall, when two mechanical knights joust, and two others play a fourteenth-century version of conkers, and Jack Blandifer kicks his heels, and Phoebe and Adam also appear (or so the Latin inscription seems to say). From the stall of the Patron of the Cathedral I could see, in a mirror, the organist's hands practicing. Then I walked out round the moat that surrounds the Bishop's Palace, and I found that this way led immediately into open country. I painted here, a view along the moat with a glimpse of the cathedral. The Palace caretaker's two little boys told me that the waterfall in my picture came from the three original "wells," in private gardens. My palette got very dirty and happened to yield just the right hornblende or manure color for the dark reflections in the water; I dabbed at an unpainted surface with a dry but dirty brush, and it looked just right for the water's bright part.

I returned to the hotel at ten. Folding doors had been locked across the passage. However, the hotel owned a garden over the street, with the purpose of preventing anyone from building there and spoiling the lucrative view of the cathedral. So I sat there and watched the hotel doors. For company I had Jack Blandiver, frolicking at the hours, and many cats. To pass the time, I wondered what I should do if she turned out to be unacceptable in some way (I had hardly seen her) and I made up a story to explain my message: I was a detective investigating the theft of the Elúnico Sapphire from the Bishop's Palace; the fingerprints of the hotel Boots had been found on a pair of shoes left outside a Palace bedroom that was no longer used, and I wanted someone to watch the Boots's movements. I put on a cloak-and-dagger expression, and a lady who came into the garden with two little dachshunds backed out and called her pets tremulously.

By this time it was midnight, I was cold, and, though open country was only just beyond the moat, I decided to take a room in the hotel. I would try to sell them my painting when I settled the bill. They gave me a room with a large oval mirror. I looked at myself, and thought, "Foolish womanhood. I would, if I were them."

Though I didn't have any footwear for him to clean, the

Boots came along and chatted with me in the morning, and I liked him. He said, "I don't know whether you're meaning to stay another night, sir, but I should tell you what them girls have in mind for you."

"What?"

"They're aiming to tie your pajamas in knots, take out the light bulb, cut off the water, put curry powder in your pillowcase, hang wool in the doorway so you think you've walked into a ghost, and make you an apple-pie bed."

"What's an apple-pie bed?"

"Why, a bed that you can't get into more than up to your knees," said the Boots as if it were common routine.

"I have no pajamas," I said, "and I don't sleep in the bed. So let them come, and we'll see who makes apple pie of who."

. . . I managed to make a sort of flat oat bread, but it was full of stone powder from the grinding . . .

. . . a hot cloudless afternoon, transparent with humidity. Beetroot-pickers lit a fire on a grassy causeway through flooded birchwoods. Within minutes the updraught caused cumulo-nimbus. Air thickened to black overhead; roaring milky whirls within it; a few huge drops; cold wind sprayed down over us and spread; the rain. Spat crackles marked small thunderclouds ignited around us by chain explosion . . .

. . . Finlaw had said that his aunt, who would like me, lived on the left side of the A 339 as it goes out of Newbury. Years passed before I followed these directions, and the A 339 now departed from a point west of Newbury, an Air Force camp having blocked its way . .

. . . after the Dutch and East Anglian floods of late 1952 I went to a house posing as a young volunteer collector for the Flood Relief Fund, hoping to get a blanket. They said they could spare a carpet, a bed, and some clothes, and would have them on the lawn for me to collect. I didn't go back. Tried to phone the real Flood Relief Fund instead, but found none had been set up yet . . .

. . . Mr. Crowe Builtisley resolved to come with me for a week. He practiced making his bed on the floor. . . . He used his gumboots as containers, stuffing them with canned food and cameras. When we got to the country, he was surprised to find the sward rough and long. He had expected it to be mown as in parks. Camping, he found, was coffee grounds embedded in the soap; a loud noise in the head as he bit grit in the bacon . . .

. . . I was gradually given all the work. Spent hours spreading foundation cream (used as gum) on picture backs with my fingers. Then the task of piecing together numbers for exhibits out of several mostly used books of lottery tickets, so that people would be forced to buy our catalog. Then I found the picture rails were very wide. The pictures hung two inches out from the walls. I could have moved all the rings in the picture backs lower, so as to change the center of balance and make the pictures slope inward. But "Fenland Artists 1959" was about to open, and they said, "Leave them swinging—they can be mobiles too" . . .

. . . sent me to some neighbors who wanted a maximum number of pictures. They had just visited Soane's Museum in London. There, pictures hang back to back on hinges on the wall so that a book of twenty is in the space of one. Impressed by this lavishness, they planned to do the same in their attic . . .

. . . in a court report in the Oxford *Daily Mail* I found my equal: "Mrs. [   ], housewife, of no fixed address" . . .

. . . some years the highest spring tide spills over the dunes of Dawlish Warren (sand bar across the mouth of the Exe) and converts the mazy hollows along the middle to a lagoon. We dragged a boat to it, moored at sundown to an islet, lit a fire and ate, sitting in our boat beside the fire. The tide came on spilling in. We cast off and drifted away. The islet was covered, the tide lifted our fire and for a time it burned floating in the darkness . . .

. . . J. B. Priestley's sister (who was staying with some ex-Bradford friends of hers called Walker): "And what about thistles? Can you eat them?" I: "Yes. Take the prickles off." "And grass? How about just grass? Has anybody tried living on grass?" "Nebuchadnezzar." She said she'd get J. B. to write a play about that . . .

greatness, no through road

I caught the chicken pox and was looked after by some
people in Kent. There were pocks in my hair, I couldn't
resist scratching them, and then I got a guilty impression
that they had released some unpleasant gas. Actually the
pipe leading to the gas fire in the room was leaky. Well,
for three years, every time I went through Kent and passed
the signpost that says "GREATNESS—NO THROUGH ROAD,"
I would stay at their house again. I always slept in the
same room, and I always noticed a light tapping noise,
like a bead on a string swinging irregularly against a
polished surface, coming to a standstill with a little drum
roll, then stirring again. It became audible only at night
when other noises had died down.

I assumed it was made by woodworms. But one time,
wondering idly whether it might be the switch of the bed
head light, hanging on a cord, I held this switch away
from the bed head. I still heard the tapping. Then I wondered whether it was coat hangers knocking together in
the wardrobe. I got out of bed and put my ear to the wardrobe. But I traced the noise to the wall separating the
room from another.

Next day I learned that a paying guest, called Audrey,
slept in that room. I mentioned the little problem to her.
She took all her clothes out of the wall cupboard, which
was on the other side of the wall at this point. We went to
bed in our respective rooms. Next day she said, "I was
so curious, I nearly came into your room to find if the

noise had stopped." "It didn't," I said. We thought perhaps it was in the chimney.

Next evening as I was drifting to sleep she came in. "I put my head in the chimney," she said. "There's no tapping noise! I believe it's in your head."

Being almost asleep, I said, "Put your head in my head" (or perhaps "in my bed").

She stayed by the door, no doubt staring. I opened my eyes, and saw she was in a nightgown and had a smut on her cheek. "There's no smuts there," I added.

She came and put her head beside mine on the pillow. She said yes, she heard it. But this was only to humor me, because actually the tapping had stopped.

. . . one day I began to talk to myself.
"PAZ *a los hombres,* GUERRA *a las*
instituciones . . . GUERRA . . . Thy
vegetable breath shall smell / Ranker than
kitchens or than hell . . ." Then a little girl
threw a stone at me . . .

. . . doss houses: if you stay awake an hour,
strange disturbances keep you for several
more. A diabetic has a faint spell and gets
up to inject himself. A man gets cramp in his
foot and staggers, clutching the wall, out
of the door to put his foot in hot water. A
crystal radio picks up a Russian broadcast
and a wall, against which the earphones are
lying, amplifies the thin sound by reflecting
it. A sleep-talker says "What hat?" Two
old men start arguing about cricket; one
accuses the other of having always bowled off
the wrong foot; the accused gets out of bed to
try his action, lopes heavily along the
middle aisle, flings his arm over, hits a light
bulb . . .

. . . driver stopped and gave me a ride in
his trailer with twenty pigs . . .

boiling boris

I knocked at a house in Ipswich, and when the ancient man who opened the door had heard my line he said: "Come in and make me a cup of tea, and after that you can do a job for me."

I went stooping where he pointed into a gloomy stone kitchen, full of steam, with a set of clothes-drying bars hanging on pulleys from the ceiling, festooned with long underdrawers, all steaming. I looked around, and he said, "Kettles on the Courtesan." He meant Courtier, the iron range that filled a low bay in the wall. On this range stood a steam iron and no fewer than four kettles, one already jumping and spitting drops which hopped away hissing. I picked it up to make the tea. The handle burned me. "You should have used the oven glove," said the old man; "that bugger's got a metal handle." I had already cooled my fingers by pinching the lobe of my ear.

He drank his tea before it had stopped rotating. When I had drunk mine, he told me what he wanted me to do: carry twelve hundredweight of coal and four of coke from the next house, where the people were moving out and selling it to him cheap. The task exhausted me and took me much of the day. Like all Bedouin, as against fellahin, I can walk forever but am no good for heavy labor.

The man next door said to me: "Old Sully's a right character, isn't he? Everyone calls him Boris, because he went to school with Boris Karloff (whose real name was Pratt). And because he looks what you might call grim."

The wife added: "Men shouldn't be allowed to be bachelors; it's too dangerous for them. The old chap's only idea of hygiene is to pour boiling water on everything. If the table gets sticky with gravy, he pours boiling water on it. The wax is ruined, the water drips into the carpet for an hour."

As I came for the next hundredweight she told me: "He's had those brick bunkers built in place of the old wooden wreck he had, but he's still got rats there. I know, because I heard one of 'em sneeze."

I tipped the coal into the bunker outside the kitchen door. Then I had to stoke the "Courtesan," first filling the coal scuttle from the bunker. I shot the scuttle too fast into the hole at the foot of the bunker, and broke my thumbnail on the bricks. By all this I earned another cup of tea, but no food, although there was the noise of fat breaking wind in the oven. But Mr. Sully became affable, and told his sad story.

He had married, and this had made his day-to-day existence relatively safe. However, he had used his wife's pinking shears on his hair with a vague idea that they would stop it from fraying, and thin it, like a barber's toothed scissors.

One day he was in the bank with his head stooped over his checkbook when he noticed a periodic noise. At first he couldn't tell how far off it was, but because it went on he traced it to a young clerk with a serious expression and a cowlick of hair. This young man had the nervous habit of clearing his throat—hardly more than a brief hum with a glottal catch—every half minute.

Time passed—the time it takes to cure a habit, let us say. Sully and his wife happened to go into the bank together. Sully heard that slight noise again. "Listen!" he whispered to his wife. "You see that clerk over there? He's got a funny nervous habit. Listen and you'll hear him make that noise again."

They listened, but the noise didn't come.

Sully's wife said, "Boris, I'm fed up with you. The things you make up about people—nasty little things, I think. I've had enough of you." A quarrel started which led to their separation.

Before leaving, I helped him fill his hot-water bottles. With one kettle I filled the stone hot-water bottle, with another kettle he filled the rubber one. Instead of pressing it flat on the table so that air wasn't trapped inside, he held the rubber thing dangling while he poured boiling water into it, so after a while it convulsed and spat over his hand. I advised him to hold the lobe of his ear.

"Why?" he said.

"It cools your fingers."

"Why?" (He said it like "Whoy?")

"I don't know, but it does."

An old woman had told me. She said that Noah blocked a leak in his Ark with a dog's nose, a woman's elbow, and the lobe of a man's ear, and that's why those three things are always cold.

We took the hot-water bottle into Mr. Sully's bedroom. It was almost as warm as the kitchen, though it contained no stove. A hot pipe ran through the wall; he made me feel how hot the wall was. "That's what I got for leaning back in me armchair," he said, showing me a burn on the back of his bald head.

Finally, Mr. Sully burned himself again (he picked up the coal shovel, which I had left dug into the ash compartment under the stove, and the blaze had made the ash hot and the ash had made the shovel hot). "Pinch your ear lobe," I said. "Nonsense—superstition," he said, shuffling round in agony. He had baggy grey clothes, and a tie round his bare neck, above a collarless shirt.

. . . had me draw his girl friend in a tennis tournament. Bought me a ticket and then I was to pretend not to know him. I was to stop them as they walked away and offer the picture; he would then buy it with ostentatious generosity. I made him be more generous than arranged . . .

. . . buffet of the Malt Shovel Inn near Birmingham. A deaf old clergyman said, "Look at that great tall fellow—look at that height! A lot of people of that height come in here." His companion, failing to silence him, came and apologized to me, returned to his place. Deaf old clergyman: "Well, what is he? Oh, a Migrant Limner. A Meager Migrant" . . .

wide-game

I read an article about Jorge Luís Borges in a magazine; Borges told his interviewer that Xul Solar, of Buenos Aires, had invented Panjuego, a game combining all games. I could not find, in encyclopedias and library catalogs, any reference to Xul Solar, and I think Borges invented him. (If you know the works of Borges, it is just as possible that someone invented Borges, or that Borges invented a man combining all men.)

Once, on a village green beside a river in Yorkshire, I was arrested by the sight of morris dancers. Then children ran a three-legged race, and a sack race, and an egg-and-spoon race. Then they ran a three-legged egg-and-spoon race. But this wasn't followed up. Xul Solar wasn't there, and nobody started a three-legged egg-and-spoon sack race.

I know about games mainly because of four times when, begging, I knocked at houses where children's parties were in progress. The first three times I was a child myself. They brushed my hair, put a clean pair of short trousers on me, and took me into a room where a dozen outline maps of islands were pinned to the walls. The guests were guessing what they were. I knew them all—Sicily, Celebes, Svalbard—and there was an impression, which I didn't contradict, that it was because I had been to them all. Besides getting the impression that *guest* was one who *guessed*, I started to *plea* when told to by one of the refined little girls—but she meant *play*.

Another time, it was Christmas, and they had balloons.

They were playing balloon ball, which combined the strokes of tennis with the tactics of football. Balloons kept popping as they touched holly. Then they sat in two rows on chairs, trying to hit a balloon over each other's heads. Then they rubbed balloons on their sleeves and made them stick to the ceiling. Then they stopped and wondered what more they could do with balloons. I said, "Why not lather them and try to shave them with razors?" Everyone was shocked. I don't know whether it was because razors were dangerous, or there was something obscene about the idea, or I ought not to have known about lather and shaving.

The third time, it was a stormy night, I had just crossed the Channel, the day seemed to have been very long, and I did not feel like games, but I was hurried upstairs to an attic where children were playing hide-and-seek. Aloof and tired, I just stood still in the middle of the room, while children hid and searched round the edges. But then, as I was the winner, I had to do the seeking next time. I found one child perching on top of a door, another in a cupboard, another barricaded behind old trunks, another clinging to the sloping tiles outside a dormer window. Then someone splashed water on me from a cistern, and a hand covered with dust reached down from a rafter and touched my face. I lost my balance, and, trying not to put my foot through the ceiling between the joists, I fell down the stairs. I spent a comfortable week at that house recovering.

After these occasions, I saw it would pay me to add to my stock in trade any party games that I heard of, so I could make myself useful other times. And I started listing them in my head:

Answering a quiz while playing round-the-table Ping-pong.

Trying to find a hidden clock by its ticking within five minutes, after which the alarm goes off.

Braying like a donkey and trying to find the one other person braying like a donkey, who then becomes your partner. (Or was that too sexual?)

"-ity"—"identity"—"president"—"Ypres"—"Donnay"—"belladonna"—"Dolabella"—"gondola"—"Oregon"—"Mysore"—"chlamys" . . . (Or was that too intellectual?)

Also I reflected on the strategy of parties: all parties, as far as I knew, were made up of three or four girls invited by the daughter and three or four boys invited by her brother; their mother arranged a series of "opening" games, after which the children expected to split off in their two groups, but the mother's aim was to make the "opening" games stretch out till there was no time for anything else. Or maybe the mother aimed to have them go off separately, but not boy with boy and girl with girl. Clearly this had to be understood if I was to be a professional assistant to the mother.

One noontime I lay down to sleep in woodland near Dowding Castle, on Walton Heath in Surrey. I was woken by rushing steps and a football punching the undergrowth. A family was playing a game they called Lurky. They drove out to this, their Lurky Spot, every weekend. One person guarded a football in the middle of the glade, they explained to me, and the others lurked nearby and tried to break cover and kick it before being touched, but if they were touched they helped to guard it. Another time, walking along a lane, I arrived at a turning at the same time as a little girl on a bicycle. She stopped, tossed a coin, and went away at top speed along the side road. It happened that this was part of a triangle where several lanes met. I saw her repeat the coin-tossing at the distant corner, and come cycling back toward me along the second side of the triangle. She arrived again at the same time as me, and again put her thumb under her coin. I asked her what she was doing. She said, "Playing a Wide-Game. We have to toss at each turning, and see how far away we get in half an hour." She tossed and, to her annoyance, had to go back the way I had come, along the third side of the triangle.

As I went along the lanes I collected conkers (horse chestnuts). Then I sold them to schoolboys at a penny for half a dozen. (I don't know whether I have to explain that they are pierced, strung, usually fire-hardened, and then used to strike each other till one conker breaks; conkers several years old have scores like 5,401, meaning that they have smashed not necessarily that number of conkers, but conkers whose scores added up to that.) One boy to my surprise bought all the conkers I had, something like fifty. He collected things, but instead of collecting one sample of each kind, he just amassed. He had several thousand matchboxes—not just matchbox labels, but whole match-boxes, and not just one of each make, but as many as he could get. He had a sackful of spent .22 cartridge cases from his school's rifle range, and a similar number of little aluminum studs left in the cuff holes of his shirts by the laundry. He used thirty of his cartridge cases, after dipping them into pots of poster paint, as the two teams in a game of Rugby football simulated on a pocket chess-board. One of the laundry studs represented the ball, being fitted into whichever cartridge case represented the man carrying the ball. The game was called Chugby Pawnball, or Chugger. For a long time I kept a carbon copy of his booklet of rules.

And I heard of more games, and thought of a few of my own to add to the list. The Wide-Game I sometimes played myself. For often, as I went to and fro across England without maps, there was no more motive to turn right than to turn left. If I was cold, I turned away from the wind; if burned, away from the sun. If I was hungry, I turned toward houses; if sleepy, away. And if none of these operated, and if it was pretty both ways or ugly both ways or uphill both ways or lonely both ways, and if I had a coin, I tossed it. Tails left, heads right; or, at a crossroads, tossing twice, two tails left, two heads right, one of each straight ahead.

The fourth children's party was at a suburban house in northwest London. The father, Mr. Stambrook, showed me straight into his study and engaged me in uneasily eager talk. He didn't want to have to go back and help in the garden. But presently his wife came in and said, "They're playing Acting Consequences now, but after that I just can't think of another thing." That was when I suggested the Wide-Game.

Not all had bicycles, so they went out on foot. I found I had in my pocket seven farthings, so they took a farthing each to toss. The only rule I forgot to mention was the half-hour time limit.

When they had gone, Mr. and Mrs. Stambrook and I sat down to tea. Mr. Stambrook was a man so polite that if any guests dropped bread and butter on their laps, he compulsively did the same.

One of the youngsters came back disgusted in less than twenty minutes—couldn't get any farther than Beresford Road. (The road we were in was C-shaped, joining Beresford Road at both ends.) Others straggled back, one of them saying she had got as far as the Watford crossroads.

By the time darkness fell, only the Stambrook boy and a girl were still out. To everyone's relief (I suppose) young Stambrook arrived in time for supper. It was his fifteenth birthday. But the girl—whose name, if I got it right, was Wendy Choe—did not.

We sat waiting. Mr. Stambrook had the radio on, and I heard that an aircraft was missing somewhere over Britain. We went out walking, hoping to meet her. I remarked, "Well, she won't be able to live on a farthing for long." Mr. Stambrook, no longer polite, told me to shut up.

I had to leave while no one was looking—against my will, for I wanted to stay and find out how wide a thing the girl had made of the Wide-Game; but I had to leave, because the police had been called. As I walked along a dark street next evening, on the southeast side of London, under beech trees, I heard an aircraft pass overhead. It crossed my mind that this was the missing one, for some reason unable to land and compelled to keep flying. In that case, I thought, the doomed pilot was very lonely up there, for all our wishing to help him.

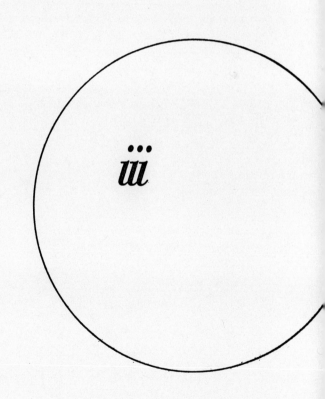

iii

That springtime I was coming down a mellow countryside
As with me through the woodland came the green returning
   tide
And the yellow sun cast yellow flowers before it far
   and wide.

But the world to me did not seem young. The land did
   not seem new.
To me each dawn was stale as dusk though pricked with
   natal dew.
Nor did I love the hazel hedge as the evening sun came
   through.

. . . there is a species of valley I call a
Miledene. "In the late afternoon we found
ourselves shut in a narrow winding
miledene. . . ." But usually straight,
about a mile long, opening out at both ends;
they had no roads in them and served as
secret routes past castles; led slantingly
through yellow-grass hillsides. Battles
developed in them . . .

. . . from Calais to Dover on the *Arromanches*
in 1951. A drunk took me up to M. Auriol,
the French president, who was on board, and
told him I could paint him. M. Auriol's
face was caked with salt . . .

. . . found children laying francs on a
railway for the train to squash. I chased the
children away and swept the francs up just
in time . . .

. . . round a corner of a lane I suddenly met
a horse running away with a woman on its
back. I shouted, "Put your hands over its
eyes!" but, stupefied, she continued clinging
to its mane, and they disappeared.
Perhaps in haste I had shouted in the
wrong language . . .

énorée

An Algerian albino took my hand in his huge wet hand
and dragged me out into the streets of Paris for what he
called a *Razzia*. The colored night multiplied in mirrors.
We carried a drunken girl to her apartment; we changed
places, I taking the head, because I was no good at fending
off the men who tried to feel her up. A taxi driver, instead of taking us where we wanted to go, halted and offered us his whisky. As my friend prepared to settle down
there, I got out. Shreds of the universal body feminine
were whirled near me out of the dark. I came to a café
where a Senegalese was drumming. People were climbing
over chairs to get nearer. Somebody wanted to dance with
me; I wanted, I think, to leave out the dancing stage; she
laughed and pushed me away. Then a woman called to me
from behind. Shouted out that she wanted me to love her.
Nobody seemed to think it odd. "He's off to fuck her,"
I heard one fag explain to another. "Oh. That's all right,
I suppose," said the other wistfully. We went down an
escalator, and she kept turning her head and smiling up at
me, while I assured her I would love her properly; and
all the time I *didn't see her*. I knew she was twice my age
—that was just the situation. Rich older woman. I could
see that her head was low down, her little face waxy,
round though bony, her eyebrows penciled and her eyes
as if stenciled through a mask. Her complexion seemed
good, but just when she turned her neck I saw seams open
in the hairy powder on it. And her suit was orange-brown.

But below that I saw nothing. I was lightheaded. I was a tribesman among flashing lights. My vision was mostly itchy frosted patches, like the beginnings of a cataract, with disconnected sparkle-edged pictures floating in between.

We went on a tram fourteen kilometers. We got off and walked across some white dust roads with ditches in them, and in among a group of shanties and poplars. There was no door across Énorée's doorway, only a curtain of plastic lace. At one position inside the room there was an unplaned post from floor to ceiling; blankets on strings stretched from it to the walls to make an enclosure for the baby. The baby was five, but an idiot. Énorée's bed had no legs, and the chair and the chest of drawers loomed over it. At least it was wide, but the mattress was of straw. Énorée was down there on it, beckoning me. What I first noticed was how dangerously thin her body was in places. Only gradually did I realize she was a dwarf. "Dear Énorée," I said, "how much do you eat?" "Only about three meals a week," she said. "Why?" "My poor hands" —she showed them to me—"too big, too clumsy for cooking." They were huge. Or, rather, they were the ordinary size, but on dwarf's wrists. I stayed with her a very long time.

. . . I was August Artist at the studios of
Extragalace . . .

. . . I did two enormous paintings on pieces
of canvas sewn together, and set them up
beside the road from Ostend to Brussels. A
man stopped and gave me sixty pounds English
for one of them, found it was too large to go in
his car, and said he would come back later
with a larger vehicle. So I had to wait that
day and the next, but he didn't reappear . . .

. . . they put me in a room behind the police
station at Gisors, but I wasn't locked in; in
fact, the door being warped, I had to shut it
with a chair. All night I heard people limping
along the corridor. The explanation was that
there were rubber mats at two-stride intervals
along the floor . .

. . . I picked a tourist spot in Metz and did
a picture of the cathedral. One trouble was
that boys dived into the Moselle just there and
often splashed my paper. Then I came back
each day and added touches, with the
aim of catching people who came and looked
over my shoulder. I would get commissions
from them, or if they were young women
I would ask them to sit down and be drawn
straight away. But if they were other than
French- or English-speaking I would not

—I couldn't face the effort of trying to
seduce in any other languages . . .

. . . man I met while rowing a boat on the
Lac Inférieur in the Bois de Boulogne sent
me to his own house to draw his mother.
He said, "You can't miss it, there's a cemetery
on the corner." It was not a cemetery
but a monumental mason's yard . . .

. . . family being arrested in the middle of
the night by a gendarme. They had slung
their Brazilian hammock—the wide kind on
which six people sleep abreast—between
lampposts . . .

. . . after a day and a half of riding with
a schoolteacher called Blanche, we came to
her town, Thann, at the edge of the Vosges,
and visited her sister, who was called,
absurdly, Mélanie. She asked what I did and
then said, "Sometimes when I see a very
large person I have an impression of waste.
Isn't all that weight unnecessary for
drawing pictures?" "Weight!" said Blanche.
"He's lighter than me!" "How do you know
he's lighter than you, Blanche?"
"Because," said Blanche without hesitation,
"we tested it on the seesaw in the
playground" . . .

. . . commuter suburbs aren't only at the
world's dull center where you live.
When the fascinating name "Oerlikon!" is
shouted, it is to the accompaniment of tram

bells as you cross contingent districts
of Zurich . . .

. . . going up in an elevator through part of
the Jungfraujoch, with an aristocratic English
lady who spoke no German. She said to
the operator: "And do they blawst the
rock?"

He could understand "And do they," he
could understand "the rock," but he could
not understand "blawst." She repeated
imperiously: "BLAWST, man, BLAWST!"

I was laughing. She turned on me and
said, "I suppose you are feeling a little silly
because of your altitude?" . . .

. . . Gerace in Italy: Tavio was a hotel
porter who wanted to be an opera singer,
so he sang to the guests. Later I met him at a
café, he wouldn't speak, I thought he was
cutting me. He wrote a note: "I got a part—
just rehearsed—resting voice" . . .

. . . joined dancing in the village hall at
Postojna on the mountains of Slovenia.
Among the Slovenian dances was one that
seemed very like the Twist. "Yes," they told
me, "five years ago the overland bus to India
got snowbound here for three days. The
tourists taught us this" . . .

. . . with other floating population I was
put into a village hall at Buchs (the place
from which there is a view of the whole
nation of Liechtenstein). There had been a

party, and about seventy balloons rested on
circular brackets, like small basketball
goals. During the night, as each balloon
shrank, it slipped through and drifted down
on us . . .

. . . "Do you like us?"—the head of an
impressive family called Testarson, in their
winter residence on the Bay of Baiae. Till that
surprising moment, I had always supposed
that it was I who was being judged . . .

. . . in Còmiso, a wretched village at
the foot of the great slope from Ragusa on its
double peak, the widow Tomlinson sat for
me. She explained her name thus: "During
the war, Mr. Tomlinson was in Tunisia, but
he got sent here by mistake. A colonel in
Sicily telegraphed, 'Send 2 D 8'; he meant
two of the tractors called D 8, but it got
changed to 'Send 258.' That was the number
of the company Mr. Tomlinson was in, so, a
hundred strong, it was shipped over here.
After two months the mistake was discovered
and the company was sent back where it
came from, but meanwhile Mr. Tomlinson
had been separated from the others and
posted with the Americans at Palermo, where
he met me. After the war we were married
in Cassibile and lived in Àvola with my
mother's cousins, and then Mr. Tomlinson
got work in the oilfield between here and
Mòdica. He died of falling and rolling down

the Mòdica street—you know what a steep
cleft that place is built in" . . .

. . . "If Abu Mahmud doesn't make his
speech at Slonta, he'll be back here with the
transformer tonight. If he gets back with the
transformer, the tape recorder will work
and Colonel Grech will hold his musical
evening. If he does, I'll go to it. If I go to it,
Mays will have to come over and be with our
grandmother. If Mays comes over to sit
with her grandmother, she won't be able to
help get ready for the wedding. If Mays
doesn't help, there won't be any baqlawa.
If there isn't going to be any baqlawa at the
wedding, I dare say Abu Mahmud won't
bother to come back for it. He'll stay and
make his speech at Slonta." A Zenonian
paradox. Either solution impossible. I had to
leave Derna before I heard which
happened . . .

morning on the myrtoon sea

From Ras-et-Tin to Ras-el-Hilal, the Cyrenaican coast remained in sight till half past three in the afternoon. Then, instead of disappearing below the horizon, it attained a whiteness inseparable from the sky.

Michael Livadaras, and his friend Ianni, and their tutor, and another Greek gentleman, and I, sat on the hatch over the larger of the ship's two holds. Both holds were empty. One of the sailors rigged an awning over us. He took an artist's pleasure in the job. Now we were sitting in a piece of stage scenery rather than a real boat. Foreground: a kind of summerhouse, in which shadowed figures sit conversing on the two gentle slopes of the hatch cover. Beyond, a sunlit gangway; the rail; the sea; the horizon; the sky. In the night, as we slept on the hatch, I woke assuming that the gentle pitching and rolling were due to machinery under the stage.

The pitching and rolling conduced to sleep—shifting our weight alternately into one set of blood vessels, then back into the other—but when we sat up they ceased to be noticeable. No one could be sick on such a flat sea. The sailors, thinking I had no food of my own, took me into their cabin and gave me a hunk of bread and a bowl of the small whole fishes they were eating. I stayed only to eat a few, because I felt slightly in danger when I couldn't see the sea.

They took a live goat on board at Derna. Its carcass

now hung in the stern and its skin dragged in the wake to be cleaned.

Michael and Ianni, both sixteen and having lived nowhere but Benghazi hitherto, were going to Athens University. They were going for five years to study *geometria*—more than just geometry, I supposed. Perhaps surveying, estate management. At the last moment on the quay Michael's mother wanted someone to take a photograph, no one had a camera, and I promised to do her a painting. But Michael and his friend were spending all day lying on the hatch, sleeping or reading comics. They were reading *Don Camillo* in Greek translation.

I ceased to notice any pitch or roll at all. The deck seemed stable, and it was the stars that trembled and slipped. They swooped in irregular trails. I looked up and saw them racing hither and thither round the masthead.

It was too hot to be in a shirt by day or in a sleeping bag at night. I had now been longer at sea than ever before. *Mediterranean.* A drain between fold-mountain lands. It didn't seem that way. No evidence but memory for any lands at all.

Captain Eleftheris, painting some woodwork, painted the nose of one of his crew red. Then he dipped his brush again, and the next moment I found that with half a red face, I was no longer such a disdained passenger.

"What direction are we sailing in?" I asked him. "Just east of north." "What speed?" "Six miles an hour." A brisk walking speed.

Rhena Dakoutros was a cement ship. (I mean it was for carrying cement.) We were to have taken several more days, calling at the island of Tenos to load with cement, and perhaps at another cement factory on Santorini; but now this was canceled.

In the early morning, everyone but an invisible helmsman sleeping, I walked to the stern and saw us pass in front of a larger ship. When it crossed behind us it was going eastward, only a mile away.

In the late afternoon someone said the mountains of Crete were visible. I could only see low cloud. At length I realized this was Crete. The far-off high land, becoming visible, does not cut the horizon, but makes its first appearance wraithlike above it.

And in the evening we passed Anticythera on our right, and waited for Cythera, birthplace of Venus, on our left. The confines of the Aegean. Somewhere under, the broken palings of the curved fence that once kept sea from sea.

I sat down on a flight of steps with a pad of paper on my knees.

> In early morning I arose and walked around
>   the ship
> And watched the time of darkness close, the
>   constellations dip.
> And everywhere the round seas roam in distant
>   mountains' lee
> And I was very far from home upon the Grecian
>   sea.

At this point I was seasick for the first time in my life. It was so quick that I didn't have time to turn my head or move the paper aside. I wiped it off. Not feeling in the least ill, I continued:

> I watched another ship; it met the day which had
>   begun

And passed across our wake and set against the
   rising sun.
I wondered who stood by its mast to gaze, and
   whether we
Should meet again and know we passed upon the
   Grecian sea.

Sunrise on Saturday found us off a land that was at
first a mere densening of the mist. It was Peloponnesus.
We were inshore of an island called Kalkoura, but inshore of us sailed another ship, a far-off fleck applied to
the base of the coast.

The high wall of mountains fell gradually away. I
realized I was looking into the Argive Gulf. We crossed
the wakes of three now invisible ships which had plied
into the gulf. But our parallel ship continued to seaward
of Spetsai and then disappeared behind Hydra. We passed
close to a rocky islet standing out from Hydra. Now midday; the rocks on the long jagged ridge of Hydra burned
in their several colors. From our position some miles out,
the towering coasts all seemed to rise vertically, but scattered white specks of houses clung to them.

I stood on the bridge. Only then could I see just how
slowly we were moving. For elsewhere I was deceived by
the swell, which still, to my surprise, ran southward. Per-
petually the water rustled past, quickly in the foreground,
slowly in the distance, thousands of grains in a rotation
about some point on the horizon. Whenever my eyes
rested on some other material—the deck, a rope, the back
of my hand—it seemed creeping the opposite way. There
was no wind. Brown-backed gulls skimmed the water as
close as water can be skimmed. Porpoises leaped, and
jellyfish inhabited the upper green of the waves.

About two o'clock we rounded the northern lighthouse of Hydra and began a due northward line which was a diagonal of the Saronic Gulf, the Thames Estuary and Hudson River of Greece. The coast of Attica withheld itself till later in the day, and the islands and peninsulas on the southern side, as we looked back at them, were now but grey silhouettes against the sun. But Aegina, in the middle, was a lovely cluster of silhouettes indeed. Large hills in the south, a pyramidal peak among them; tumbled hills in the center around a valley sliding out to the sea, and long wooded ridges in the north. As the ship crawled past, I gazed hard at Aegina, home of the Myrmidons and the Aeacids, little island that once shared the world's trade with Athens. So I was actually here, sailing through ideal Greece of interlocking sounds and mountains.

Now Attica: shipyards along the foot of Hymettus; the Acropolis and other monumented crags seeming to stand not far back from the water up a wide urban gradient. The Piraeus, sprawling over a group of promontories, expanded as darkness fell, for chains and clusters of lights came out round the bases of yet farther promontories. Gradually we came to a standstill between the port and Salamis, too late to land this third night.

The crew gave me a supper of *bamia*. I wasn't sure whether these were vegetable shoots or octopus tentacles. They made the Greek boys, Mike and Ianni, ill, and through the night, each time I got up to fetch them a drink of water, I first went to the rail and reoriented myself. What is around me? Water; and around the water? Greece; that way: Aegina; that way: Athens.

Soon after dawn we began to move; passed Psyttaleia; Cynosura with lighthouse; through one of the two winding channels that make Koulouri, or Salamis, an island, into an enclosed basin half water and half plain. Along the dividing shore, Eleusis, the city of the Mysteries; the Eleusinian Mysteries. But now it is the grimy little city of a monster cement factory, and that was why we came to it.

We passed at anchorage our sister cement ship, the *Antonios*, and the *Almeria*, another vessel on which I had once had it in mind to come from North Africa.

Sunday, so no customs men could be persuaded to come aboard till nearly noon. Captain Eleftheris raised his final price from six to seven Libyan pounds; Mr. Hatzidakis found a friend to change my remaining three pounds at sixty-five drachmas each instead of the official eighty-two; Mr. Hatzidakis and Mike Livadaras (still sick) took me in their taxi to Athens. Thirty miles, they said it was, but it did not seem fifteen. Through the gap in the Aigaleos hills, where Daphni monastery lies, and from then on we were in Athens; for the modern city fills nearly all the plain that in its great times was a whole country.

The first thing I did was buy a copy of a subversive newspaper called the *Vima*. In it I found the results of a lottery held thirty-two years earlier.

. . . keep sunflower seeds till they sprout—
more nutritive then . . .

. . . Mr. Sabuncuoğlu ("soapsterson"),
descendant of an old governor called
Caratheodory Pasha, has a house on the
Princes' Islands and a shower with four
nozzles, so that water tans you all sides. I
went to sleep, slipped to the floor of the
narrow tile cage. Pats of water smacking on
water seemed rain shafts blittering on awash
pavements of a more wintry latitude.
They dragged me out, my hair was so clean
it squeaked . . .

. . . passing along the Hellespont in a ship, I
made to the peasant woman standing beside me
some remark about the scenery. She replied
merely, *"Menderes gitti"*—"Menderes
has gone."
    I was taken to a prison and shown men
standing in cells which fill as the
tide comes in . . .

. . . the salt deserts of Iran are the only
absolute deserts. Not even insects live in
them. The Daryache-ye-Namak, "little lake of
salt"—I was not really in the middle of it,
but in the fringe, not far from the Tehran-
Kashan road. After seeing the sun set, I took
it into my head to turn about and wait
watching till it should rise again on the other

horizon of the white sheet. Decided to do it
on my knees, and see how it was for ascetics,
and knights at their vigils. The first of many
things I saw was an aircraft still sunlit,
traveling west. It was as if the pilot had
chosen the most beautiful moment and was
keeping up with it, and would come over again
after the sun . . .

. . . rock reefs that interrupt the lunar
plain south of the Elburz are full of colors so
contrasting that you think there are
cloud shadows and sun; but there is no
shadow. A beggar lives in the overhang of a
bank where the road cuts over one of these
outcrops. Taxi drivers, caravans, and
pilgrims to Qom give him coins. He told me
his name was Owni and he had been running
away with his wife's cousin when God
struck him, at this spot, with giddiness, eleven
years ago . . .

. . . leaving an Afghan village just after dark
I met a Volkswagen with a CD for
Corps Diplomatique and FL for Fürstentum
Liechtenstein. Two men got out wearing Boy
Scout uniforms. They were Prince Emanuel
and his nephew Prince Franz, cousins of
the reigning prince. The uncle, who said
"Just call me Emanuel of Liechtenstein," was
Chief Scout of the principality. They had
driven to a jamboree in Delhi, stayed
everywhere with ministers and millionaires,
and had no need of the mass of canned food

in the back of the car, under the bed where
one slept while the other drove. They sold it
all to me for two hundred afghanis, and I
buried it, meaning to transport it somehow to
Ghazni and sell it for two thousand . . .

. . . but at dawn I met Powindahs on the
move. Two hundred camels carried swaying
mounds of luggage, with children or
cages of poultry strapped to the summits;
rifle-bearing men and unveiled women
walked, silhouetted against a hazy sun. These
were a section of the great Ghilzai tribe of
Pathans, who in the eighteenth century
overran Iran, and who still nomadize each
winter into the Indus Valley, whence their
men go on, even as far as Australia, mending
cauldrons and peddling dirty postcards.
For a gift of canned food I traveled with
them eight days . . .

. . . "You ought to have some patter,"
said Promilla from Lahore. "You ought to
crack jokes, or say 'Cheese' like a
photographer. Why don't you tell me
stories?" I said I couldn't think of two things
at once. "Well, shall I tell you stories?"
"Not till I've finished your mouth." So while
I rendered her sari she told me a string
of Elephant Stories: Why-does-an-elephant-
have-yellow-soles-so-that-he-can-hide-
upside-down-in-the-custard, What-does-an-
elephant-do-when-he's-stuck-at-the-top-

of-a-tree-he-sits-on-a-leaf-and-waits-for-
autumn, What-is-red-and-lies-in-a-ditch-a-
dead-bus, What-is-small-and-white-and-
carries-a-trunk-a-mouse-going-on-holiday,
What-is-small-and-brown-and-carries-a-trunk-
a-mouse-coming-back-from-holiday . . .

. . . this did not happen except in my
imagination: A count, margrave, or raja
wants nudes to decorate his castle. I say,
"Leave me here alone for a week with a girl,
a larder, hot and cold water, paper and
charcoal, and I will provide forty square
yards." I fulfill this, but he complains: "She
wasn't very lively." The case was that she
was so lively I had no chance to draw her
except asleep. To compensate I write him a
song beginning:

> She's a girl so very frisky making love
>   to her is risky,
> She's a girl so very sweet you wouldn't
>   think she's made of meat . . .

. . . I had thought that if I saw a girl artist
I would say, "You're a masterpiece though
your picture isn't." By the Temple of Sunium
as I passed a rock I found a girl behind it,
using it as a desk. The wind was in the act
of turning her folder inside out and
touching her cheek with it. Her painting was
so good that I went on without saying a
word. Later, seeing unframed watercolors

heaped on a landing outside a garret gallery,
I learned that her name was Vicki Miien . . .

. . . got a dictionary in Greece. After hard
use its spine came away and revealed part of
the text of a treaty used in the binding.
Signatories were KAMTINI MTSHABA, ELIAS
MVOKOZELI, TEMBANI MTSHABA, and the feet
of MAMAKAZI MTSHABA . . .

. . . I never knew you could eat nettles till
village women at Umm Qeis in Jordan
showed me how to gather them. I thought of
them as enemies to slash aside, to grasp firmly
so they wouldn't sting, or if they did sting
to counter with dock leaves . . .

. . . a Bank of England employee. He
urged me to buy a suit and work there too,
because there was only one person in the
whole outfit who knew Arabic . .

. . . when I say that I got across country from
the sea to Shiraz, I simply expect you
to understand . . .

. . . at some unknown time in the night
(though Tashkent is due north of Kabul, its
clock is an hour and a half later, while
Moscow's is an hour and a half earlier) we
entered a magnificent Tupolev jet and set out
to chase the sun. There was no vibration, and
nothing but darkness to see through the
window. At some even less known time, I woke.
Everything was still. Everyone else was

sleeping, yet the plane was standing on a flat meadow of grassy tufts, covered by snow and illuminated by a yellow moon.

The meadow was made of cloud, and the little tufts were cloudy domes perhaps miles in height . . .

girl with russet scarf

We ate *befstroganov*, read the Moscow *News* from cover to cover, and were taken to our plane about noon. There were only four of us for Helsinki. One was a girl with her hair covered by a russet scarf. Her appearance was noble, because of her tallness and the modesty or expressionlessness of her face, which was light brown and so regularly shaped that I could not see where its distinctiveness lay.

The Kremlin was a shadowy mountain on the horizon as we took off. I was at a window on the left; the girl with the russet scarf was at a window on the right. I wondered whether she was Russian, Finnish, or perhaps Estonian— through a break in the clouds I saw what must have been the shore of a lake on the border of Estonia and Russia. Most of the time the tundra of clouds was unbroken, but I thought to myself: "Though pleasurable moments depend on moods, flying makes them almost inevitable. Its only drawback is that it gets you to the end so soon." Then someone brought me a tray of food, and then I looked down, reading something, for half an hour.

We bumped down one step of air, and I looked out and saw we were over the sea, in which were five or six low flat islands, and boats near one of them. The Finnish coast came into sight, far ahead and below. It looked like a multitude of pebbles mingling with the water. Over it, tall white clouds were massed. They cast elongated reflections in the tideless and waveless gulf. They were like trees standing at the pebbly brink of a stream. The plane dipped; fragments of cloud raced in front of the fragments of land, to make a teasingly complex kaleidoscope. We were told to fasten our seat belts.

Instead, the girl with the russet scarf stood up and lurched across the corridor to me—put one knee on the seat beside me, and leaned across me to the window, saying something which must have been "Excuse me" in some language. There was no room for my head at the window. I did think of offering to change places, but I was seatbelted in, the time was short, and I looked at her instead. Her brown skirt was ungracefully long—she was old-fashioned. Her profile was like a queen on a coin.

She burst out talking to me, in German, about what she could see. I couldn't understand at first; then I gathered we were passing over property owned by her father. She told me to look, and past her head and arm I saw that the pebbles had become forested islands, with some clearings, houses, and roads. Jetties projected from the beachless rocky shores, where the water was so still that in enclosed bays it was stagnant. There was no boundary between sea and mainland, but a medley of water and land, like a pattern formed by paint crumbling off a wall. Farther inland the terrain undulated a little, and there were rivers with parallel banks. All the countryside seemed designed, model-like, by someone looking down from an aircraft. I didn't like to insert my face too close by hers at the window. I drew back, and looked again at the daughter of a rich father. My memory is of more laughter than seemed characteristic, and a whiter cheek. At last I kissed this cheek. How could I not, when it was so long suspended just there? She stood back, looking punishment at me (and lurching again, so this obviously was not what she had planned). I replied with a little sound of plaintiveness, which I should not have done, because it alerted the other passengers to what had happened.

A succession of smiling uniformed girls guided us into an airport building which looked completely unsoiled by use. A passenger said, "Why, this is Western Europe again, the Land of Reason!" And indeed the people were mostly Nordic, the faucets worked in expected ways, and the alphabet was clear. The town was twenty kilometers away. My whole resources at that time consisted of one English pound, which I changed for eight hundred and ninety Finnish marks. The fare on the bus to town was a hundred and fifty, so while the others got into it I set out walking. The countryside seemed all created recently, on a plan. Signs in Swedish and Finnish tried to tell me what everything was. I had wondered whether Finns would show any traces of Mongoloid origin, but I couldn't see any. I had read somewhere that slant eyes, like dimples in the chin, must be inherited if either of the parents has them. But there were more blond types here than in Sweden or anywhere else.

The British Consulate was on the seventh floor of an office block. I had heard that consuls would help destitutes to get work on ships, and I intended to try this. A Finnish secretary was first sent out to see what I wanted, and I said, "To borrow money." I thought that if the consul thought me a sufficient nuisance he might strike a bargain. He appeared then behind a counter, to keep me at a distance; said he could only get working passages on ships for discharged sailors; suggested that I telegraph for money to my bank—"If you have a bank." He meant that as a really exceptional snub. My own parting shot was to ask him if I could sleep on the floor in a spare room (I could already see it was out of the question). He didn't answer that, but went on telling me that a telegram would cost me four hundred and fifty-six marks for twenty-two words.

A short stout man had been standing near me, filling in forms and smoking a cheroot, and he followed me down the stairs. "Come with me," he said. "I'm living in a hostel where you can sleep." I said I really had no need of that, and would sleep in a park. But he went on about the hostel, explaining that the beds were full but he had two outsiders sleeping on the floor last night, unknown to the landlady. We knocked on the door till the landlady came, and we went through a ritual of begging her to let me in. She said she could not; my friend pointed out that the other bed in his room was empty; she said that, as he knew, the man who had it had gone away for a few days and was paying for the bed to keep it; my friend asked if I could sleep on the floor; she said no; he asked if we could telephone the other hostels; she said no. All the while, she was trying to escape back into her kitchen, so we finally let her. Then we went ahead into the bedroom. My friend told me he had to pay four hundred marks a night, and asked me for two hundred. He explained that his name was Marty Leftwich, and he was a student of architecture. That was why he had come to Finland: it has the best modern architecture in Europe—he mentioned the stadium where the 1952 Olympics were held, as an example. He had been here nearly two years, and now he was working in an architect's office. They were creating a kind of fun palace, including boathouses and a sauna bath, on the estate of a man called Forsala, not far from Helsinki. He claimed the firm had got the job because he, Leftwich, had picked up Forsala's daughter at a dance. Now, this evening, he had to go out and meet her and smooth things over, because she had just got back after four months abroad and he had failed to meet her at the airport with his car. "What am I going to tell her?" he asked me. "What reason am I going to give for not being there?" "I don't know," I said. "What is the reason?" "The real reason is that it's cold and also I didn't plan to buy petrol till Tuesday" he said. "But I can't tell her that." I suggested he might tell her he had accidentally driven his car into a lake, but he told me Finland is not all lakes.

When he had gone out I stayed in the room, because if I went out I could not get back in. I got under the top blanket of Leftwich's bed, so that if the landlady came in she might think I was he. I was ready to sleep anyway, since I had come from far to the east, where the day had ended earlier.

About midnight Leftwich returned with the girl, Signy, who was still wearing her russet scarf. They had been drinking, and their entry was noisy; they switched the light on. She was a foot taller than he. I was to be the last feature in the evening's entertainment. The girl had come deliberately to see me, since she realized from Leftwich's description that I was the person who had kissed her on the plane; and Leftwich thought it a good idea to pose as (among other things) a sporting fellow who had smuggled a tramp into the hostel. "Let's go and see him, let's go and wake him up!" they had exclaimed to each other in the town. "Are you game?" "Oh, he's taken my bed over!" said Leftwich as he came in. Then he spotted *Don Quixote* lying on the floor. For it was only just before this that I had been given the book, which, ever since, I have loved more than any other; and I had been reading it in airplanes and before going to sleep. "Sit up and read it," said Leftwich. I obliged, and they were gratified at the sight of Don Quixote reading *Don Quixote.* I had just started having pain from a wisdom tooth, my first, and that perhaps made my face look more gaunt. Leftwich picked up a cardboard tube (containing an architectural drawing) and, couching it under his armpit, made a wobbly charge at me. I wished I were drunk like the other two.

The antique dignity which was Signy's very substance did not sort well with drunken behavior, of course—but no behavior did. Her dignity, which expressed itself most purely in her appearance, was a ceiling from which there could be no movement but downward: she could have stayed perfect only by doing nothing—anything she said or did was liable to fall short of the expected dignity. I saw the drunkenness as the necessary step she had to take before coming here. It wasn't that she was afraid of coming into a men's hostel, or afraid of the landlady, any more than she was afraid of walking about in an airplane when her seat belt was supposed to be fastened, and being rebuked by a stewardess. Her authority (she no doubt felt) rose above anyone who might try to rebuke her. It's amazing how secure a tall young person with light hair and a rich father can feel. But to burst in here at this hour in order to see me would have been less dignified sober than drunk. She hadn't spoken yet.

"Well, so you kissed her cheek," said Leftwich.

I said to her: "I think even a person who wasn't in love with you would have kissed you then."

She asked Leftwich what I had said. He told her, slowly, in Swedish, which he had learned.

"What do you mean by being in love with me?" she asked me in German.

"At least I worship you," I said, or thought I said. *Wenigstens ehre ich dich.*

Leftwich woke me at five o'clock, saying "It'll be safest for you to clear out now. The old woman gets up pretty early. Go down the hill outside and you'll find a café open on the left. The cheapest thing to eat is *kaurapuuro* and *maito*, porridge and milk."

Helsinki felt cold. It is farther north than the north of Scotland, and I had just come from farther south than the south of Italy. And it was September, so I had also flown from summer into winter. The trees were turning color in the Kaivopuisto, or Brunnsparken. A few people were by the quays or on park benches to watch the dazzling morning sun climb above the sea. It was hard to believe that the water was sea and not a lake. Mallard ducks sat on it. I dipped my finger in it and found it was hardly salty. Helsinki is on an irregular peninsula, surrounded by subsidiary peninsulas and islands, and I walked slowly all round its shores. I had no adventure, except when I followed some other people across a narrow bridge by which a single line of a railway crossed some docks, and just after we got to the end of the bridge the train came.

I went by elevator up the tower of the Olympic stadium that Leftwich had mentioned. Somewhere I saw the sign of "oy FORSALA ab" (which is to say, "FORSALA, Ltd."). I got to the end of *Don Quixote* and (not for the last time) started again. I sent, to the person who had given me the book, a postcard, in bad handwriting, because my fingers were cold. When I wanted to eat again, I could not interpret the items on the price list other than *kaurapuwro* and *maito,* so I lifted the lids of saucepans in the kitchen and pointed. A slightly drunken sailor came and sat on the edge of my table and talked to me in thick English, or German, or Swedish; whatever it was, it kept me entertained for a couple of hours without need of meaning. I tried to ask him whether he thought I could work on his ship, but he answered with a kind of lump of verbal ore which I could mold into anything I wished. Such German as I knew was coming back to me, although when I wanted to say "yes," "or," and "but," I kept saying *bale, ya* and *amma,* Persian words.

What I was meant to be doing with the day was finding a way to earn money, as I had only a hundred marks left— enough to buy only a pair of socks, which I nearly did, my feet were so cold. But the thought that I might exploit the girl, get her father to let me paint murals in his sauna baths—this thought, having once occurred, robbed me of my will to knock on doors. My strange behavior to her might even help, since I was an artist and not an architect. Pictures don't have to stand on sound foundations.

At the end of the afternoon I returned to the hostel, at the same time as Marty, coming from his work. He let me in, but he didn't speak. I had expected to spend the evening listening to his talk. But it was clear he was in no mood for that. He glared at me with plain hostility. After a time, he fell to just thinking gloomily. I read his Finnish dictionary. Then, as I had nothing else to do, I got into my sleeping bag on the floor and shut my eyes. But every so often I apprehensively opened them again. He sat with his spherical head enclosed in his hands like a football. His frizzy black hair seemed to be wearing away because of his fingers worriedly pushing up into it. The light stayed on. His black boots stayed heavily on the floor boards. He had sometimes worn green shades, and I wondered whether I would be more disconcerted if he wore them now, or less.

He thought on and on, sometimes allowing a glance for me, but mostly, I think, inwardly frantic in one of those neurotic mazes where every consideration conspires to increase misery by making it more subtle. An extra stroke of a whip merely *adds* pain, and everyone can understand that, measure that, sympathize with that— they ask you how many tears are appropriate, and you just say how many whip strokes you suffered. But these neurotic thoughts do not *add* pain. Each of them gives a subtler dimension to the pain, or casts doubt on the pain, or shuts off an escape from the pain, or removes a reason for sympathizing with the pain, or makes the pain igno- minious, or makes it less easy to describe the pain. For each thought is so felicitous, so much of the material of dramas, that you feel you must tell it. But each is unfair, and short of its full force, by itself; so each requires the qualification and explanation of others; and they, of others. But each connects with more than two of the other thoughts, thus making it impossible to arrange them in linear order. So, if it ever all comes out, it will be a vast, tortuous, refined, grey mass, which no one will want to listen to, or read. This was what Marty was experiencing, for I could see that there were things that made it impos- sible to stay in my presence, and other things that made it impossible for him to go anywhere else. All he could do was keep silent.

We were in the fifth or sixth hour of this state when we heard a handclap. Once I made my home in a building that had been demolished. It rose in three terraces up a slope from the street, and I slept on the middle terrace, behind a half-standing wall, stowing my bag in a hooded fireplace. All the other buildings round about had also been demolished, except for the walls of the back alleys, which ran between them, and one house. The bricks that had tied it to its neighbors stuck out raggedly, and most of the roof slates were gone. Several times each day and night the old man came out, in his shirt sleeves and braces, and clapped. He did it to drive away the pigeons, so they wouldn't shit on his house. Partly asleep, I thought it was this old man I heard clapping again.

But the next thing I knew, Marty had brought the tall girl into the room. It had been her imperious clap out in the yard. She still wore her russet scarf over her hair.

She gave me one silent look and then spoke to "Martti." When she had finished, he motioned me to get up out of my sleeping bag and sit on the opposite bed.

"I'm to be the interpreter," he said.

She spoke Swedish flatly, without its tonal lilt. Her accent was probably very poor.

"She says," said Marty, "that she has come to tell you that she wants to give herself to you."

Then he listened to what she had to say next, and with more difficulty translated:

"She says that she's come at the time itself, rather than making any appointments. She's going to give herself to you now. I hope you want her now."

Then with the next installment he had difficulty over a word and had to work it out with her.

"She says she is a virgin," he said, "though she is twenty-six. She says she expects it to be quite graceful. . . ."

I was blushing as if strangled. But she was just standing with her back to the door.

"She says she will go out of the room, and you will lie down on the bed naked. Then she will come back naked and lie down with you.

"She says don't stroke her, tickle her, kiss her, or something else. Just go into her. Oh, you may look into her eyes and smile, but not speak.

"Then, she says, shut your eyes until she's gone."

"Anything more?" I asked, for Marty's last bit was shorter than hers.

Pause.

"Other times, she says, it can be different; just this time she wants it to be this way."

Looking up at her, I realized I had never imagined any nakedness inside her clothes, as I had never imagined her hair without the russet scarf.

She opened the door and went out. There was a small dark area outside, between wooden doors; from one of them the landlady might come; behind others men were sleeping. It would not have mattered to her if it had been even the street. Our room was the theater; the rest of the world was merely undressing room. Any ruffian or landlady who happened to burst in would have been waved back with no feeling beyond impatience.

"Well, follow instructions," said Marty.

I did so, stiffly. I only had underclothes to take off. The wait after this embraced more seconds than I liked.

"Remember, she wants you to *glide* into her," said Marty maliciously.

I wondered why he had not slipped me something extra during his translation, such as "She says she doesn't like you, and is doing it because—" Not enough imagination to complete it, perhaps.

He stayed sitting on his bed. He had been given no other instructions.

I thought to myself: "He must have looked forward to marrying her, but she must think of him as a gnome. . . . I hope I *do* meet the parent who brought up a girl to be such as this. . . . Knowing the literal things which are usually hidden till last, such as how fucking is done, but not the nebulous social feelings. . . . Perhaps I'll be impotent with her. Easier for a camel to pass through a needle's eye than for a rich man's daughter . . . Yes, secretly an ordeal, and that's why we want to be alone. The death of the bull is made terrible by the spectators. . . ."

She opened the door and came in naked except for her russet scarf. This she left in its place, either because she was so used to it that she forgot all about it or because she would seem different to me without it. Never have I seen such a naked body. Yet it was regularly and almost dully shaped, slightly larger than the average, firm and the same light yellow-brown as her face. Her breasts were small and narrow like her nose. A slight shininess marked the ridges on either side of her belly. It was as if Love itself were uncased; no titillating details were necessary to the awe. Her head scarf made her unscarved body yet more naked, and yet reminded me that there is something else, besides nakedness, to naked people.

She came naked into the room, lay down beside me. It took place as simply as the accidents of the flesh allow. Then I shut my eyes and rolled aside, felt the bed lift after her and heard her close the door, but never saw her again.

A couple of days later, when I could no longer wait in Helsinki, I set out walking westward. I thought there must be some way to get from island to island across to Sweden, since there is no open sea, only a gradation from lakeland to archipelago and then to lakeland again. A car with reindeer antlers tied to the roof stopped beside me; it was driven by a pharmacist, who took me to Salo, a village that, he said, was just about to reach the status of a town. He treated me to *paistettu makkara*, sausage meat with gravy, potatoes, and beetroot. Just after he had driven off, I found I had left *Don Quixote* in his car. I was very sorry, but have had two other copies since.

. . . remembered and wanted to return to the
Wood of Thrushes (so I called it). Stream
full of islands, thrushes running about,
plump and blond like grass spiders. Through
the trees, a glint on sheets of tin rattling over
the chief forester's peas.

I found it. But the thrushes were all gone,
wiped out by eating things with insecticide in
them. So now snails multiplied; after the
dew, forty of them dotted the glade like dog
droppings, others climbed my tent . . .

. . . Groningen: I had an address, but when
I asked two policemen standing by the
encircling canal, they said they were from
the province, didn't know the town, and could
only direct me to its center. A man befriended
me by the Martinikerk, walked with me
past the A-kerk, and pointed to a house across
the water: "If you have your own sheet,
Mevrouw Boerema will let you sleep there."
The door opened with no one behind it; the
Mevrouw had pulled the latch by a rope
from the stairtop. She gave me a breakfast of
chocolate beads on bread and set a visitors'
book before me. I saw that the last visitors had
drawn a map of their future route round
Europe, so I drew one of my past route round
Europe, Africa, and Asia, but then tore it
out and just wrote "Jecon" . . .

. . . cover your eyebrows with your forefingers and look in the mirror: you are a stranger. Amorot was a farmer whose likeness I had drawn and who had said, "If you ever pass this way again, remember my doors are never locked." When I did, I wondered why he looked so different. He said, "My wife was unfaithful and I cut her hair off. It's grown again now. She fixed a better revenge for me: singed my eyebrows off with a primus stove. They never grow again—well, more slowly than a little toenail, and a man can't use eyebrow pencil" . . .

tea-drinking in many lands

I—je—ego—icon—jegotism . . .

When I was tired of a room and lessons, I went to the beach, taking a second set of clothes with a diary in the pocket. I left them and went away. The Sunday newspaper published a report two weeks later that I had possibly been eaten by sharks. It happened that one had been washed ashore in Bournemouth Bay the same day.

There was always afterward a problem, as they say, of identity.

In Europe, Poste Restante; in America, General Delivery; kept only fifteen days; sent on to the downtown office; mispigeonholed under "E" for "Esq." . . .

Once there was a letter for me but I couldn't have it because it had been addressed to "His Loneliness Lord Jecon of the Paths."

There was a serviceman in Trieste who was editing a newspaper for the American troops there. He interviewed me and half filled two issues with my answers. He was going to pay me, but I didn't want a lot of Italian money, because I had been told that the canals of Venice give rise to a stench in the summer, and I intended to move north. He sent a money order for me to a lady who ran a small radio station in what had been, till a couple of years before, the British, French, and American zones of Austria. He had studied with her at the Sorbonne. Her name was

Franca, but now she was in Austria she spelled it Franke. He told me to be thinking of themes I might broadcast about.

Don said he came from a place called Sandy Ague. Or maybe Sandy Ego. He was always talking too fast to spell it out. He had already arranged a Fulbright scholarship for himself to come back and research into Venetian history. He talked in notes for his dissertation, somewhat like this: "Enetoi (originally with a digamma, FENETOI, Wenetoi) mentioned by Homer in Asia Minor. Veneti lived in northeast Italy, probably of Illyrian origin. Hence ancient writers thought the leader of the Enetoi migrated to Italy after the Trojan war, like Aeneas. The region being Venetia, the town—at first a refugee village in the marshes at the fall of Rome—must have taken its name from the region. Surprising, seeing that even when powerful Venice avoided dealings with the mainland . . . Adige Valley equals South Tyrol. Includes most of the southward bulge of the Alps. Bilingual. Trento or Trient; Egno or Neumarkt; Bolzano or Bozen; Isarco or Eisack; Bressanone or Brixen; Mezzaselva or Mittewald . . . Used to belong to Austria. Now two provinces: Trentino is around the straight Val Lagarino; Alto Adige is the valleys radiating to the passes in the Alps. These being easy, especially the Brenner, this has been the usual funnel for invaders. Latins, Umbrians, Sabellians; Gauls under Brennus; Langobardi; Austrians. Invaders who came by other routes (Hannibal, Cimbri, and Teutones, Ostrogoths) did not stick. . . . As you have come from Slavonic land, you must lodge on the Riva degli Schiavoni. Once, by the way, the doge forbade people to use that name because it reminded Slavs of their servile origin. But Slav can't be derived from slave, because of the proud Slavonic names like Jaroslav and Slavko—in fact, it's the Slavonic word for 'word'—but Serb must be derived from *servus,* as that's definitely a Latin word for slave. If there had never been slavery, what would we fantasy about? The *degli* before Schiavoni seems to show the Italians think the s is 'impure.' If you take my advice and stay with Biondo, he'll be happy to show you all those churches with famous paintings. At the doors you'll see one of those notices about short sleeves et cetera: it says, 'Do not shock the children.' " And then he made a careful joke. "Did that enlighten you about me?" he asked. I said yes. He said, "The problem we have is enlightening without frightening."

He drove me to Monfalcone along the narrow hilly strip of Italy before the plain of Friuli. No cars go into Venice; having crossed by the causeway from Mestre they are put into a five-story parking structure, the first I ever saw. Within the city, no vehicle except the speedboats tearing up the water of the canals, and the gondolas they buffet aside. No traffic accidents because no traffic. No through streets; only little bridges linking the tangle of one island to the tangle of the next. Guessing is no good for finding the way, and I hardly ever felt certain where I was or what I would see next. Venice did stink, but I hope one day every city will be like it.

From Tripoli I had written to the Esso Service, Paris, asking them to send maps of Greece, Yugoslavia, Austria, Belgium, Netherlands, Luxembourg, to me at Poste Restante, Fondaco dei Tedeschi, Venice. To my surprise, they did, and I had to pick up a parcel of maps so heavy that all I could do with it was drop it in the Grand Canal. Before dawn when I was leaving, the five-thousand-car parking structure was almost empty and a certain noise spilled out of all its concrete windows. A boy was careering from top to bottom, down all the ramps and among the pillars, on one of the things that eight years later in America were called skate boards. Perhaps when the age of the burning of oil has been brought to an end, all parking structures will be playgrounds.

The tourists, the latest wave of German invaders, were going home for their elections on the 15th of September, 1957. Five men, one of them a priest, returning from Taormina to Berlin, offered me a ride in their car. They were talking about how to get rid of small cash. "It doesn't pay to have bits left when you cross a border; you lose at every exchange. Isn't that so?" they asked me. It was, for the Greeks had said my Libyan money was no good, Yugoslavs said Greek money was no good, Italians said Yugoslav money was no good. "That's right! Deutsche marks are the only hard currency. We have only five thousand lire left. We're going to spend them on either a meal or a woman, in Trient or Bozen, and then get out of Italy quick. How much do you have?" I only had one lira.

We came to the Brenner, hardly a pass at all, just part of a grassy valley. On a cliff beyond the summit was painted "Freiheit für Südtirol!" We got out to look at this. There was drizzle, and I felt the cold. The Germans said, "See, there's a little booth over there. Why don't you go see if you can spend your lira on a candy?" I went and asked if there was anything for one Italian lira. The Germans started up their car and left me. They passed with a hearty laugh at their joke: they had taken (perhaps by accident) my bag, with such papers and currencies as I had, but they had left me a pair of roller skates.

It was not unfunny and it was not unpractical: after all, I was on top of the Alps, and it was downhill all the way to

Innsbruck. I roller-skated about four miles and then stopped to look over a fence at a blonde girl who was driving one of two tractors round and round a field that swelled up over the valley floor; as one tractor disappeared the other would appear. She wore a swimsuit; the flesh of her forearms bounced as she went past me, and sometimes she had to stop and struggle with refractory gear levers. She called to me, "The bus is coming. I see it." The bus came and went. "Why didn't you get on it?" "Because I'm still talking with you." "Idiot! There isn't another bus all day." When she had finished harrowing the field she told me to hold the back of the tractor, and she pulled me the rest of the twenty miles to Innsbruck. In the dusk we descended a long winding road above a tributary of the Inn, and the lights came into view like a flood along the floor of the main valley: *"Tschungejungejunge!"* she exclaimed, as she had done at each fine prospect. My roller skates howled all the way; as soon as we came to a standstill, the first thing I heard was again "Idiot!" (". . . *ein Holzkopf* . . .") from a passer-by.

I found the address of Franke; it was a cottage completely dominated by a transmitting aerial in the back yard. But as I was some days early I wandered away and back again. It was raining in Landeck, it was raining in Strengen, St. Anton, Arlberg, Liechtenstein. I tried to think of themes to broadcast about; I also tried to devise proof of my identity. All I could think of was to send some letters to myself at Poste Restante, Innsbruck, with begged stamps and with addresses in pencil; when the official let me have them (which he should not have done) I erased the addresses and got several people at a youth hostel to write other addresses on, without the name; then I forged my name with their pens in their handwriting. One wrote a name by mistake, so I wrote "Care of" in front of it. Before calling on Franke, I looked again at this ridiculous evidence—this bunch of letters that looked as if they had been franked and delivered to me at places with funny names all over Austria—and I threw them away, though I was tempted to keep the letters and notes I had written to the irresponsible Jecon from sundry long-suffering men and women.

"How," said Franke, "am I *te jeconnaître*—to jecognize you?"

The rest of it went something like this: "You pop up like a Jecon-the-box—how do I know whether you're Dr. Jecon or Mr. Hyde? You seem to have the genuine jeconoia—practice jeconomy of words—but do you know the jeconine secrets? You may be nothing but a second Gregory, jeconsequent upon the first. . . . If I give you Jecon's shekels and you're nothing but a jecho, a jeconical projection, a jecongregoria of the imagination, that would be most objeconable jeconoclasm, wouldn't it? Have you any proof of your identity?" She poked her finger into my nose, and when I involuntarily pushed her off she fetched out this letter to show me:

> . . . Jecon is vague and probably has no documents on him, or they're in some other name. In case you're afraid it is somebody else, let me tell you three physical details which, taken together, must be unique:
> —The septum of his nose is crooked, making a convexity in the right nostril (no doubt early efforts to breathe past this are the reason why the nostrils are somewhat flared).

—There is a small bony process on the
front of the left collarbone just before it
meets the shoulder.
　　—There is an even smaller lump in the skin where
it lies in the pit below the lower end of the
breastbone. You can tell this lump is part of the
skin because it moves when you move the skin. . . .

"*Mon ami Don est-il un* fag?" she said. I didn't know
this American word; to me it meant a cigarette.

"This morning," Franke said, "Dr. Dromann, who was
going to record something for our Women's Hour, sneezed
and lost his voice; so we can use you." The studio was
like an aquarium between two soundproof windows where
technicians watched me. I had to talk for an hour on something that would suit English-speaking ladies. The only
theme I hit on was tea: Tea-Drinking in Many Lands.
Franke looked disappointed, but the technicians were already counting down to the next figure on the clock. I said:
In Morocco, mint tea. Ordinary mint, but a special kind of
tea. The glasses have thick bases so as not to scald your
fingers. People told me cardamom in mint tea would be
good for my dysentery. In Israel: infusing bags in the
restaurants, in the kibbutzim cold tea extract and hot (not
boiling) water. In Iran: the blocks of sugar are snipped up
with scissors, then you hold a lump between your teeth
and drink the tea through it. In Afghanistan: you receive
a bowl and a pot of tea. All the bowls and teapots hang on
the teahouse wall: red bowls and pots for ordinary tea,
blue bowls and pots for green tea. You pour yourself two
or three bowlfuls; in the bottom of your bowl when it is
given to you is your ration of sugar, which is granulated,

imported from Russia, scarce, so you mustn't stir or there won't be any sugar for your second bowlful.

In Uzbekistan I found a plum at the bottom of my teacup. It made no difference to the taste; it was just there. *Chai s slivkami* is Russian for "tea with cream" and *chai s slivami* would be "tea with plums," but I certainly didn't say either.

Maté is thick green tea stewed with much sugar; picked by tribes of Indians who travel forever with their tents through the tea forests of the Chaco. On those Channel steamers that are operated by British Railways, tea is ready-made in an urn with milk and sugar—any French passengers have to eat it that way. . . .

At one stage of my life it had even seemed to me that questions were insults. If I wanted to state some fact—to strike out all but one of some set of possibilities—I would do so; a question could only be on what I had not volunteered. At a yet more silent stage, questions became essential. If I hadn't been asked anything, I would never have said anything.

Now I was spouting about tea: . . . in England, a lady brought a pot of tea and I picked it up and poured it into the sugar bowl. "You think you're in Marxistan, do you, or wherever it is they drink tea out of sugar bowls? What were you thinking of?" "Nothing." She pressed me till I said I had been thinking about—morphophonemics. "When you're thinking about morphophonemics," she said, "lie down on the floor, will you? That's the safest place when you're thinking about morphophonemics." And that reminded me of the time I lit a gas burner with a match and then put the matchbox on it instead of the kettle. . . .

I went on to record another talk, on passes (the Bolan

Pass, Pear Tree Pass, Ice Pass, and Shipka Pass, the Cilician Gates, Honister Hause, and the Pass of Glencoe; how in Cyrenaica "pass" meant not a notch but a place where the road zigzags up a step in the land, and how you often encounter people at the top of passes and can sit down beside them pretending to be breathless also—hence the expression *making passes*) and I had a debate about the Suez crisis of the previous year, with a German, and about General Mikhailovich of Yugoslavia with a British officer. Don't know how many were ever broadcast. After the last one I said to Franke, who was the moderator, "I wanted to make one more comment, but you wouldn't let me." "It was the clock that wouldn't let you," she said. "The clock made the last comment!"

. . . I met Ernest Thesiger, the greatest living traveler, stopping at a hotel in southern Spain. He wore a grey suit and carried one small suitcase . . .

. . . Ezequiel, looking at my legs, trying to pick me up: *"No me importaría morir entre las columnas de ese tiemplo."*

Later, familiar, kidding me: *"Caballo grande, ande o no ande."*

Idris, at my innocence of practical wisdom: *"Man lam 'allamahul-abawaani, yu'allimhul-malawaani"*—Him whom his two parents have not taught, the two times (night and day) will teach . . .

. . . after I had painted him, Father Maisje took a photograph of me and said he would paint me from it, and add finishing touches when I came back. When I did, he complained that I was fatter in the face . . .

. . . as sunset approached they told me we were crossing the border of Ostfriesland, the part of ancient Frisia that belongs to Germany, and that Frisia was the second democratic republic in existence, after Iceland. In exchange for this I pointed to the places where the various stars would appear. "Ah, the stars!" said Mrs. Griencke. "You have the clouds to study by day—then the stars to console for the loss of daylight—then again the dew to replace the stars." "There isn't much thrill left in them," said her father, "if you can point to them by day" . . .

. . . got yet a fifth set of pastels in Holland, because I liked their names: Groene Aarde (terre-verte), Paul Veron-Grün, Smaragdgroen/ Chromoxydgrün (viridian), Scharlakenrood/ Scharlach, Hellrosa . . .

. . . stream called the Yesto dried up in one night. I stepped into it to see if fish were lying about. But there had been heavy rain higher up and the stream had temporarily dammed itself with uprooted bushes. Flash flood came, swept me round two bends, I clung to a rosebay . . .

wild-duckling chase

About nine years ago at Lyons I framed my pictures, sold some of them, and left the rest in the gallery. I moved southward. Six days' journey down the gorge and through the "Tap of Provence," a great canal was being finished and I worked on it. The work was too hard for me, and I left without collecting my money. I slept once under a bridge, connecting nothing to nothing over nothing in uninhabited country. The French don't knock buildings down when they have finished with them. In the region to the left of the Rhone are whole empty villages. I lived in one by myself for many days, and was bitten by an adder. A little natural-holed flint that I found on a floor where I had slept proved that the deserted laithe had once been a stable; for such holeystones, hung up by string never cut or changed, guarded the horses from being hag-ridden. When the string rotted, the holeystone fell. I could take it to guard me from starvation. Only on the last day did I stir myself to make drawings. I hurried on down to Avignon. I took the way through L'Isle-sur-la-Sorgue. On a stream were people passing in a punt, and they carried me the rest of the way. At Avignon I went into a hotel, and got one sitter to paint, but the hotel was stuffy and the sitter sleepy and I soon wanted to leave. When I spoke of deserted villages, someone told me of Les Baux, and I went there. It is an empty village and fortress on a terrific crag, and bauxite is named after it. But it has many tourists. In the deep green valley at its side is a hotel, where I worked in the laundry. Honeymooners came there, and one could get large tips. When I left, I was attracted by the little range of rocks called the Montagnette, and camped in a crevice of them. Other such sharp islets —the Alpilles, Montmajour, Beaucaire—stand in this plain of mud. Hordes of insects swam on their backs like sharks, and men walked rapidly backward in the water planting rice. Where there was not water, there was long grass and reeds and maize and the windbreaks of cane or cypress. By a salt lagoon I slept on the flat crown of an Italian stone pine—the stem had no surface of its own, so studded with burly boughs that I could walk up like stairs; pushing through the roof of needles (and having to leave my basket hanging below) I spread a blanket, passed a string round myself, and tied its end to twigs. Returning to Avignon, I had a more prosperous time. I went to Tarascon to do drawings of the open space by the waterfront for a man who had a scheme of founding a university there; pleased another man by detecting his Dutch accent, and he took me to one of the Chateauneuf-du-Pape *domaines,* of which he was manager; sold cups of tea in the street to English tourists who insisted on asking for it in cafés, where they found it cost them ten shillings; watched an oil tanker, struggling up the Rhone past the Pont d'Avignon, suddenly be defeated and start moving backward. It was raining all the time, so that when I quit Avignon and looked back on it from the Tower of Philippe le Bel in Villeneuve I saw one of the most beautiful of all sights: the sun, about to set, dropped below the roof of clouds, and struck the Palace of the Popes and Mont Ventoux and the silver undersides of the leaves all the way along the wooded islands dividing the river.

I walked west to the Pont du Gard and to Uzès, where

a cycle race passed through. The cyclists had traveled four hundred kilometers but were suddenly brought into a bunch by an old man in a Bath chair who got in their way. A bundle of sixteen newspapers hit my shin, thrown from a music-blaring van—the local newspaper and the Philips Razor Company were sponsoring the race. There was also a band setting out to march to Nîmes for a festival, but when I walked with them a short way they became motorized. At Nîmes just then Hitler's armored car was on view. I was in the square watching children roller-skating when one of them climbed on a public weighing machine and tried to make himself weigh more by pressing upward; something went wrong, and he did himself an injury. I carried him to his house. His parents invited me to stay, but soon the neighbors sent a policeman to see who the dirty stranger was, and I left. Outside Nîmes I saw a car with a Moroccan number plate standing by a farmhouse. I was tempted, and waited some hours for the driver to come out. But he told me he wouldn't give me a ride because there had just been two murders by hitchhikers. And the next time I stayed in a house was at Perpignan (in the Rue de Père Pigne) and it caught fire. Thus I was reminded not to depart from my ways—always walking, always sleeping in the open.

I must move faster. At Gerona I lodged with a prostitute. Her stories of the Civil War made me feel more and more burdened with responsibility to record them, till she told me they had already been used by a novelist. In Barcelona the truck that watered the streets in the morning watered my basket, which I had left standing, and all the pictures I had were ruined. Someone gave me his book of kilometric tickets for the railway; three thousand kilometers, in five-kilometer coupons, and there were twenty-five hundred kilometers left. I soon understood why he had given them away. I was penned for fourteen hours in a compartment with a dozen other people—a sickly bullfighter sleeping on my shoulder, a hearty German, a pauper with trousers held together by clothes pegs, a man with a dog in a bag, others reading American comics, and a yellow-haired, green-eyed Visigoth with lips cracked and skin peeled by the climate after all these centuries. The only way I could rest was to climb into the narrow space over the corridor. A woman on a platform begged for coins and got only an insult, so she took out her breast and flung a splash of milk all across the window; no one after that would open it. As soon as we got to Madrid I gave my kilometric tickets to someone else (twenty-three hundred still left). I walked to the city's western brink, where the Plaza de la Armería between cathedral and palace looks out over a wooded slope to the pleateau of New Castile and the distant rim of Old Castile, and I had that feeling which the issue from a city always gives. But I thought I ought first to go back and study the Prado; I did (I've never seen so many people copying—each had his permit on his easel —one was even copying a copy of the Mona Lisa) and then the usual adventures enveloped and detained me.

Rosarita Rosares, who is no longer alive to mind my saying her lovely name, made for me a nest among the swallows' nests in Toledo. From my ledge I looked straight down on the ruins of Cervantes's house. Toledo is a dead old city with a lively village flourishing in its middle. Bursting life huddles in the Calle del Comercio and the kite-shaped Zocodover; from this side, our building was a government office, entered through a Moorish arch. Ruined houses, separated by irregular slopes of earth instead of by streets, clothe the descents to the encircling river across which the besiegers bombarded in the Civil War; it was from this side that I came in at ten o'clock each night and found my way up to the fifth floor, where we dined on a balcony in the warm air. As I came up the steps and through the room that led to the balcony, I would hear a great hum: the people in the Zocodover. We would eat, looking down on them as they slowly circulated. Then I added to or changed, according to the experiences of the day, my Interpretation of Toledo, a kind of map in tempera. Lines came from the mazes of my own movements, blocks from my ideas of the balances between districts—high or low, flat or steep, old or new, brown, narrow, erotic, snobbish. Districts changed color, and magnified as their details impressed me. If I had stayed long enough, the map might have become merely accurate. Afterward, I saw such sketch maps in every lonely rocky region I camped in, in the bends of the Guadiana and the valleys of the Sierra Morena, but having a table to work on for a time had made me lazy.

I came into Córdoba in the middle of one night. I walked all over it while there were no people in it, and looked at its naked shape. It was the cleanest city I had ever seen, and as white as a bone. I felt like an archaeologist in some Cretan maze that had suddenly reconstructed itself and brushed itself for him. The sun came up, and still I walked for hours through suburbs, looking at cleanliness and prosperity without people—lanes freshly blacked between walls freshly whitewashed, churches as yellow irregular piles at the corners, red flowers, gates open into luxuriant patios. Still without seeing any people, I moved in among numberless pillars supporting horseshoe arches. I could see that this low hall was vast but could not see how vast, because sporadic chapels and altars interrupted the views. Then I saw rich red curtains. As I came toward them they were taken down, suddenly revealing the space of the cathedral pushing up through the roof of the mosque. Women sitting on the floor were mending the curtains—the first living creatures I saw in Córdoba.

I didn't stop in the town by day, but went with some boys who drove donkeys through the water to marshy islands in the middle of the Guadalquivir. A boy, starting from the Spanish way of prolonging final vowels in downward glides, passed into a long Andalucian song, each phrase beginning as if abruptly spoken, then going into tremulous held notes.

Among places I slept in after this: olive groves full of jays; the bed of a stupendous river gorge made dry by two dams.

When I got to San Roque and was in the café, gathering interest and letting it be known that I make portraits, someone jokingly suggested I should paint Ri and Milcíades—two schoolmasters who, it seemed, didn't want their faces on paper. When we knocked on their door they were both in pajamas at midday. It was now definite that I should paint a full-length picture of them robed like Jacob in many colors. I began, surrounded by ironic youths. While I tried to draw, all argued bitterly at me over Gibraltar (the people of San Roque are refugees from it) and "Ini" (Ifni) and "Paña" (Spain), though I told them I held no brief for the British government. When the pupils had all gone, these two men told me that what they really thought was different, since they could not smuggle if they had no Gibraltar. They had been smuggling all night, and that was why they were in pajamas. They invited me to join them in a simple operation.

We went to Gibraltar next day, stayed only long enough to change some pounds to pesetas at the Gibraltar rate of fifteen hundred instead of the Spanish rate of eleven seventy, and left on the five o'clock ferry taking Spanish employees home to Algeciras. Nearly everyone had a bag of cigarettes, watches, and such. As the boat sailed across the bay, they stuffed these goods in their shoes, hats, sleeves. The women, in loose black clothes, had extra capacity, and Ri and Milcíades were selling more contraband to them. Milcíades strapped things round his arms with elastic, and took his trousers down to strap them round his waist as well. At Algeciras I started through the barriers with the Spaniards, and before I was stopped and sent round with the non-Spaniards I saw customs officials plucking articles from each man as he passed—like fruit from a tree—and dropping them into great garbage cans that stood by for the purpose. Sometimes there are more thorough searches too, but enough gets through for a profit.

Milcíades tried to recruit me for the smuggling trade. He told me how the women push jewelry into parts of their bodies. He said, "These British have an Armistice Day on November the 11th, with a two-minute silence. We had a man who was trying to go into Gibraltar; he said he had nothing to declare and they chalked their marks on his bag. He was just going to walk through, when the two-minute silence started. Everyone stood still for two minutes and listened to things ticking inside his bag. At the end of the silence he was arrested. Hispe, his name was."

We were conversing in a hotel in Algeciras; Milcíades was in his pajamas again, and he had brought a pet duckling with him. It was walking about on the table. Suddenly it got my eyelash in its beak and gave what seemed to me a severe tug. In my fright I seized it, and it died in my hand. Milcíades seemed to forgive me.

Ri and Milcíades found a tanker in which we could cross to Tangier more cheaply than in the ferry. But I tangled with officials, and my two friends went without me. I went over to Tangier on the ferry (told I could stay only one hour because I had no vaccinations, but of course I took no notice of that). In Tangier I allowed myself to be taken to a "hotel" because it offered both hashish and girls—the combination was too much. We slept in wooden chicken pens on the roof (rats clattering over their corrugated iron lids) and woke covered with swollen bites which lasted a week. I did a story-mural in a restaurant. But part was on the inside of the door, and that door is always kept open on the street.

After a few days the smugglers found me again. They were engaged in manipulating pesetas and Hassanis (currencies the government was then trying to suppress in favor of Moroccan francs). They got me to take part in an exercise. We left our café, strolled across the marine road and the railway line onto the beach, and joined a group of men with sacks of wheat. The remaining restrictions between Tangier and the rest of Morocco were on money and wheat, and there was a customs inspection before the train left the station. The train came slowly out. Men were leaning out of the doors with left arms outstretched. We had to hold the sacks up to them. They ran inside with the sacks, stowed them under seats, and came back for more. When all the sacks were on board, the train-borne part of the team jumped off into the sand. Then—and only then— the train gathered speed and curved away into the interior.

Another time I was asked to be on the train, and I found it exhilarating, hanging on by one hand and grabbing sacks, and looking forward to the leap and tumble. I ran into a compartment where a man (wearing a sombrero over a turban, as is not uncommon in Tangier) impassively read a newspaper and lifted his legs as I pushed the sacks under his seat. But I undertook one sack too many, and couldn't jump off. Life began again, with a new basket and new colors bought in Fez.

In the plain of Sais between Fez and Knes (as I heard Meknes pronounced) lookouts made of poles and straw towered over the fields; they had either sentinels or dummies in them. I climbed one for the view, but it contained a sentinel, not a dummy; I was taken before the great landowner, and ended doing his portrait and that of his concubine. Hospitality, as usual, lasted several days. In the forest of Mamora, said to be the largest troop of cork oaks in the world, I was in a glade by the road when two hitchhikers were set down beside me by a car that was turning off. They were a Canadian boy and an Australian girl, traveling on a thousand francs a day. We ate, and while the boy was out of earshot the girl told me he was bullying her. She wanted to join me because I seemed gentler. I told her I walked, not hitchhiked. But she said she would wait for me at Rabat. I reached Rabat a couple of days later. Moll was not at what I thought was the youth hostel (it was really the Service des Sports et de la Jeunesse). The seaward half of the area within the city walls is a cemetery, and I slept there. I rose before dawn to paint as many pictures as I could before people were about (I did four: a rush-roofed street, a street like a drain, the view over the medina on one side, and the river on the other from the crenelations surrounding the garden that leads to the Casbah of the Udaya). I took these to the fashionable open-air café on the tip of the Udaya Casbah and walked round showing them till I got a commission. On Friday I went to join the crowd filling the great space between the royal palace and the mosque, waiting to see Mohammed V pass for the noon prayers. There came troops on horse and foot, in white and red, then notables, then the sultan in a coach; the men clapped, the women made their tremolo ululations; the sultan passed between a line of musicians and a line of old men bowing; the coach drove into one of the doors, and came out without the sultan; the muezzin appeared on the minaret, and could just be heard above the wind, the singing beggars, and the tinkling of the men selling water from sheepskins. I looked at the overflow of worshipers in the colonnade, prostrating themselves when the wave of prostration passed out from the interior, and at the women in their separate wing of the building—and among these I saw Moll. She had gone native by putting on the veil. (In Morocco it is supported by the tip of the nose and doesn't hide the eyes.) When the prayers ended and the sultan rode out on horseback under a parasol, Moll made her way to me with a group of women, who plucked off their veils (one with especial relief, because she had to wear glasses absurdly over it) and revealed themselves as very chic types: Madame Moweilihi from Lebanon, her two sisters, three daughters, and a cousin. They had helped Moll in some trouble, and afterward offered her the usual hospitality at the house they were renting in the sister city, Salé. The family driver took us to the edge of the Bu Regreg River, and we crossed in a little square boat under a white awning, rowed in Maltese fashion by a standing man facing forward, to a beach that stretched inland. All bathed, and at their insistence I too bathed, wearing the lower half of the cousin's bikini. The Moweilihi ladies recounted—and re-enacted

—the trouble from which they rescued Moll. "While she was bathing, the police confiscated her clothes and put them in a locker. Then, she left her swimsuit on a rock to dry, and it was stolen. We went to the police station with her (we saw a German there, arrested for stealing a swastika-shaped key from the Musée des Antiquités). But wasn't it lucky the two things didn't happen to Moll at the same time?" With that, the daughters ran away with my clothes, and the cousin pulled the string on the side of her bikini and whisked it off. The only thing I could do was lie down. They tried to turn me over or burrow under me, and then tickled me with streams of sand. This was supposed to encourage Moll.

We went along the riverbank to the Little Harbor Gate, formerly a water gate, leading into a sunken area which once was a harbor but is now the mellah (the Jewish quarter); from there, through the Haja Gate to the seafront garden city where the Moweilihis lived among all the Europeans. That night, Moll made love so limply that when she was asleep I went out to find something else in the mellah. Salé too is half cemetery, and I spent the rest of the night there, more comfortable in the open.

In Rabat I tried to learn club-juggling from a traveling entertainer, but broke the chandelier in his hotel. I also tried to learn a cure by sitting each day at the feet of an old man in the Swiqa, who expounded from a dirty old book and a picture of Adam and Eve. I asked him so many questions to which I couldn't understand the answers that he told me I ought first to learn Arabic properly, and gave me the newspaper *Manar el-Maghrib* ("Lighthouse of Morocco") which had vowels printed for learners. I found myself reading about an "Austrian" (me) wanted for indecent exposure on the holy day. Returning to the house,

I noticed a police telegram in French to "Mme. Mouilhi."
It was time for me and Moll to get out of Rabat. She told
me what an ideal country Morocco is for hitchhiking, because the towns are a hundred kilometers apart, with
nothing much in between, so you can get from one to the
next each morning and sight-see in the afternoon. This
kind of travel did not appeal to me at all. I told her to go
by bus and keep a place for me at Casablanca.

I left Rabat by the Gate of the Winds and, sleeping an
hour in each of the wooded ravines the road crossed, instead of sleeping at night, reached Casablanca in two days.
But it was long enough for things to happen to Moll that
convinced her this wouldn't work. We went to the port to
find her a ship back to Europe, and I wanted to work my
way on a ship to the Canaries, and then to Dakar, so I
could resume my way round Africa on land. We found a
group of people like us, waiting for ships they would
probably not get: one who had been laid off a ship for
getting a poisoned toe from a splinter on the deck, two
others working for their consulate while they waited,
another who got a place on a French ship but lost it when
the captain found he was Swiss not French, another who had
had his passport confiscated and his money stolen, another
cheerfully expecting a ship for Sweden. Where could we
live while we waited? In the city, I couldn't use sex to find
free lodgings for both of us; if we went into the country
and camped, she would have to walk in with me each day.
She went to the youth hostel, and I slept in docks, shrines,
among the rocks by the sea, *en famille* in a suburb called
el-Hank, and sometimes slipped into the hostel at night.
By day, Moll shifted buttons on my clothes (I was thinner
from Moroccan dysentery). She called me Pine Cone
Jecon because she found a pine cone that she said looked

like me. I put it by the fire to open and yield its nuts, but all we got was the incense scent of burning resin. I earned some money by guiding tourists, rubbing a wonderful lotion (vinegar) on their mosquito bites, and advising them how to live cheaper—telling them the minimum prices and to buy glassfuls of unsugared yogurt (not the hygienic date-stamped kind) and grapes that had been broken from the stalks and rancid *smin* instead of the ordinary butter *zibda*, weighed out instead of in packages. Surprisingly, people were mean enough to pay for such hints. I even earned an American cent by telling a man he could use "Moroccan toothpicks" (a common little plant that looks like the stamen bundles of camellias but is stiff) instead of dental floss.

Tired of waiting for ships, we set out hitchhiking. When we were out in the country and nobody had passed for an hour or two, she would tuck her shirt round her waist and take off her bra to sun-bathe. She used to stand with her arms folded behind her back as if pinioned.

There was a French hotel owner, with his Moorish employee sitting on top of the stock of drink they had just bought; and then a van filled with loaves except for the front seat—we were so squashed that the driver's hat fell out of the window, but he didn't stop for it. It was Monday, and he was taking his loaves to Suq Tnin Shtuka, the Monday Market of the Shtuka people. At siesta time there seemed no hope of another ride, so we got on the bus for Mazagan. An old man in the seat behind us collapsed. Amid deafening advice, the driver reversed to the old man's hamlet, and the old man was taken out and laid on the ground, where he died. A woman waved her hands in the air and slapped them on her thighs, uttering long wails that ended in yelps, and soon wailing women came from all sides. One vomited. Six men brought a rough bier (a plank with two sides and with two handles at each end), and the old man was carried away with his tribe following. We stopped at a police station on the outskirts of Mazagan, and I and four other witnesses made statements. Asked for an address, I could momentarily think of not a single English street name.

Feeling, as a bus passenger, unusually respectable, I asked a policeman for permission to camp somewhere in Mazagan, and to my surprise he accompanied us and had us camping on the *terre-pleins*, the artificial land extending into the sea for port installations not then built. One day we helped the people who collect seaweed on the rocks beyond the city—the men bringing it in sacks to the earthen avenue between the city ramparts and the Jewish cemetery, the women there spreading it to dry. The next day we went to the sale of Mazagan horses on top of the dunes between the beach and the road to Azemmur, and wondered whether horses were the answer to our problem —Moll had lost her taste for riding in buses, where men either died or were too lively. We made our way back to Casablanca, and there, instead of hoping for ships, frequented the European community and enquired for someone driving all the way to Europe and needing a companion. We found a Belgian physical-training teacher, but he changed his mind and stayed at a Moroccan school. We found a Moroccan Negro (a blackamoor, in fact) who was going to flee the country before his antiroyalist and anti-French views got him in trouble (one of the things he told us was, "Before the French occupation, Germans came here to learn from us how to make rifles; *ergo*, if the French had never come, we would have been the discoverers of the atomic bomb!") but he got jailed. Finally we found a Polish doctor who had worked twelve years in the Anti-Atlas, curing eye diseases, syphilis, and tuberculosis, and was leaving because he took a depressed view of Morocco's independence—"*Ce pays va retomber dans le primitif!*" I told him to treat Moll as a wife, no less, during the journey. I hoped that would ensure his temperateness, if not disinterest. Moll asked me how she could let me know if she did marry him. I could think of no way.

While we were at Casablanca, among the people awaiting ships for Dakar or Sweden, I had looked at a map belonging to one of them, and I noticed that Morocco is studded with names like Suq el-Had Isa, Suq et-Tnin Imin-Tit, Suq et-Tleta Uled Fares, Suq el-Arbaa bil-Gharb, Suq el-Khemis Zemamra, Suq es-Sebt Uled Hassin. Now *had, tnin, tleta, arbaa, khemis, sebt* are *one, two, three* . . . but they are also the days of the week, so these names meant Sunday Market of Jesus (a local saint), Monday Market of the Gate of the Eye (in Berber), Tuesday Market of the Children of Fares, Wednesday Market in the West. . . . (There were no Friday markets.) Each tribal district had its market village, and in each the market was on a different day, so that merchants could move from one to the next. I bought a map and followed this routine. I knew at which village, each day, I could find the tent-covered booths formed into a square, or pitched in the middle of a square of outward-and-inward-facing shops, and the battered cars and trucks lining the roads nearby; and among the local people with their money ready to spend, or the merchants who had just made their sales, I could always find someone to buy a picture or barter food for it, or some group who laughingly commissioned a portrait of one of their elders. Two or three sales, even for very little money, make me rich, since I spend almost nothing. There were things that the map didn't tell me: Sidi Smain was a Monday market, Suq el-Jemaa Uled Teima seemed from its name to be a Friday market but the market was on Thursday; at Suq et-Tleta Sidi Bu-Gedra nothing was happening on Tuesday, for the market was at nearby Tleta Sidi Mbarek. In this way I passed through the region called the Dukkala and came to Safi, the port with the largest sardine fisheries in the world, but, for all that, a quaint little town tapering up a slope between two mighty walls.

The dusk promenade fills the main street through the medina and, beyond a three-arched gate, spills into the Valley of Shaaba outside the northern wall. This valley is like a moat to the city, clothed in sloping concrete terraces. Here a shooting gallery and other stalls were set up as in a fairground, but the greatest crowds surrounded groups of entertainers without any stalls. One ring formed round a man with an assortment of objects on the ground and others in his hands; he talked vigorously, staring hypnotically in front of him, and sometimes exchanged objects with people in the crowd. I could never make out what was going on here. Another ring surrounded a bespectacled and befezzed gentleman with a hand drum and a young man with a lute. At first they merely talked in a desultory way, occasionally sounding a note or two on their instruments, or using them for mime, or engaging in banter with the crowd. Gradually they began to play and sing. They stopped, and the lutanist took the drum and the drummer took the lute. The young man settled into a long impromptu song. When a beggar woman pushed her way into the circle, he adapted a few stanzas to her. These people collected no money.

The third crowd surrounded the greatest theater I have ever assisted at. In one end of the clear space were three men, playing and singing. The middle man had a lute; on his right was a man with a hand drum and a high penetrating tenor voice, dressed as a woman; on his left, also with a hand drum, was an awkward oaf in a tattered cloak —me. I had been spotted sitting on a bridge, drawing, and had been pressed into this part. At the other end of the space was a little man doing a shuffling dance, smiling and singing back at us, and gesturing with a tray he carried. He moved around the ring collecting coins. One man stepped into the ring to give a coin, but wanted change, and was left to delve for it in a leather wallet lying on the ground. The lutanist recited between bars of music; then the performance gradually assumed the form of a drama. People in the crowd shouted suggestions about what should happen next. The man with the tray picked up a toy sword and danced more fiercely. His tray of coins was passed to the nearest onlookers, who passed it along to me, and I used it as a tambourine, passing my drum to the crowd. A second lutanist appeared. A young man in a long white robe and white skullcap stepped in and executed a stiff dance in front of us, rotating slowly, shuffling his feet, rarely changing the attitude of his arms, and all the time his face was a perfect blank. The music finished in a climax, with performers and onlookers (if such a distinction can be made) shouting and clapping. We broke up with a cry of *"El-hamdu-lillah!"*—"Praise to God!"— from the chief lutanist, and slipped away over a footbridge to a small gate in the wall and into the medina to his house. He told me that an artist came to Safi and made a pictorial plan of the medina some years back, climbing on the roofs of the houses to see what they looked like from above. As long as I stayed with this host, he forbade me to buy any food, even *taking my money from me* so I wouldn't disobey him. He couldn't conceive of a non-Moroccan and, classifying me as a Fasi, cooked me meals in the style, he said, of Fez—lentils in gravy, *kifta* of beef and eggs and tomatoes, hot sugared milk.

I had another traveling companion, from a place called Tamanar. He was the French proprietor of a café where I stopped for a drink. On the wall a framed clipping showed the sultan with microphones and a caption: *" 'Considérez le Maroc comme votre propre pays,' dit le souverain aux Français de l'empire chérifien."* The Frenchman told me Tamanar was insufferably hot, the nearest water was five kilometers away, there were only ten other Europeans there (I was surprised there were so many)—and he asked me why he had stayed at such a place twelve years? He vowed he would come with me, and put his boots on and took a gun. As we walked along the road, he told me every possible reason in the world for suicide. Finally he turned round and went back to Tamanar.

Some days later, after meeting advance detachments of fog among the foothills, the immense beaches, the scarps, the occasional rich valleys, I rounded Cape Gir and at once saw a dozen fishing vessels scattered over the southern sea. Agadir was at that time a shapeless place strung over six kilometers of coast, cut by ravines into four sections, but without a medina or any other center. A couple of years later it vanished in an earthquake. Though it was almost the southernmost place I had ever been (as well as westernmost) it was under a Londonian fog. Cold, I crept at night into a space in the side of a building. There was a noise of voices and a light switched on, and I was looking through a crack onto a stage where students were rehearsing a dialect Arabic comedy, with much shouting and slapstick, and cries of "Stop!" (in English) from the producer.

The fishermen of Agadir told me they never sail to the Canaries. When I got away from the cloud that sat on the town, I found that the waste places of the Sous Valley actually grew turf—the best sleeping I had had for months. At Ait Mellul I wanted to take the fork of the road that led on south toward Ifni and the desert, but here my courage failed and I began the swing back to the north.

Days in the plain of Sous . . . sleeping with nothing on or over me so the mosquitoes would have plenty of choice before biting my face; sleeping in places where I could see the stars, the Atlas, the Anti-Atlas, and any light or fire in the plain for forty kilometers; sleeping on a roof with a guard and his rifle and half a dozen traveling women; woken at dawn by a donkey passing my head, and finding nine Moors sleeping round me on the concrete steps of a gas station; walking amid dusty columns of donkeys coming from market; helping the daughter of a village carry one kettle over the hill to the spring. There was no question of pictures here—in the houses the usual loyal and pious pictures were reduced to the single word "Allah" printed on a card or daubed on the wall. (Yet once I met, doing his devotions under the orange trees, a scholar famous all over the Muslim world.) But there was no need for money either. Bridge-menders gave me grapes; on going into a roadhouse and taking my place on the rush mats in the courtyard, I would receive a glass of coffee for ten francs (in other words, as a gift) and refills would be free; they would arrange a luxurious night for me by finding two sacks of straw and propping the smaller one up with a stone so they would be level. The people were mixed Arab and Berber. The strange Berber architecture of white or pink mud, with zigzag crenelations and tapering square towers, culminated in Tarudant, a city like a great toy.

At Tafingult the plain ended, and I met people on bicycles sailing down from the pass of Tizi-n-Test. The road took thirty complicated kilometers to reach the top, scaling the final wall of rock in three long loops. In a café at the top, a German hitchhiker had waited three days for a ride. Now came the long and wild descent, through mountains of alternating red-to-mauve rock and silvery green rock, and glens full of flowers and white squirrels in the dirty ringlets of blue Atlas cedars. The road was rock and grit, all my pastel colors were shaken to bits in my basket on wheels, vehicles miles off down the gorges sent columns of dust eddying up the hillsides in forms like inverted waterfalls. Down to the level of rhododendrons and of Berber hamlets like stacks of matchboxes or like Tibetan lamaseries: each was in color exactly the same as the soil from which it sprang, and in form almost the same as the terraced fields around it. Then at the top of the level of trees, the castle of Tinmel. From here the Almohades went out to conquer the "world" (that is, Spain). This region, though so near to Marrakesh, had always been stubbornly independent—and, when you have seen the country, it is little wonder. On down past eroded red valleys, the valleys funneling into gorges, the gorges overhung with castles, roads chipped into the gorge sides, and wreckage of taxis crashed into the rock. And out into the plain, battered by warm winds.

I slept among orchards and vegetable plots in the Aguedal, the great garden that stretches three kilometers south from Marrakesh. Bounding the city are three *meshwars,* or parade grounds, and after a dawn wash in a reedy pool in one of them I went in through the Bab Berrima, where Jewish craftsmen were beating scrap metal into flat strips. Marrakesh (Mraksh, its people call it) is a clean place, full of a scent like incense from the little braziers of men selling tea or cooking kebabs (here called *kutban*); full also of private processions and the noise of drumming in the streets; of pathetic madmen with a disease that bends both joints of their left arms, little drums on their wrists which they beat as they beg; full of beggars' calls from the mere word "Allah" to epic chants. Often one beggar indites verses, while another—or a whole choir of beggars sitting on the ground—intones the refrain. Men sitting over tea in rush-matted rooms pass the time by clapping in leisurely rhythms, just like groups that one finds behind banks in the countryside. Muezzins of little mosques without minarets call from their door-ways. After dark, a muezzin standing on the roof of his mosque, having finished his call, extinguishes his light and vanishes like a ghost. I never even looked out of the gate leading to the *ville nouvelle.* The three other tradi-tional capitals of Morocco (Fez, Meknes, and Rabat) are real cities, and so are many lesser places, but Marrakesh is not: it is country and desert life, temporarily pegged down between walls but always ready to drift away. I made use of a weekly market like those of the country, held both outside and inside Bab el-Khemis, the Thursday Gate. The center of the medina is the Jemaa el-Fna, like a dusty country *suq,* a rag of ground famous for its musi-cians, snake charmers, acrobats, storytellers. People would greet me with *"Haben Sie kein deutschen Brief-marken?"* or "Hey, Fritz, want to take our photo?" My hair was bleached by the sun, but there are plenty of blond tall blue-eyed long-faced Berbers, and with only a slight change in my ragged clothes the tourists would have been photographing me.

A group gathered to watch a left-handed man rapidly and beautifully painting a sign on a shop window: *"Et-ta'mīn jamī' el-akhtār,"* "Insurance against all risks." I said it should be *Ta'mīn jamī' el-akhtār.* The argument about classical Arabic was settled (in my favor) by knocking at the gate of a learned man, the custodian of one of the shrines of the Sebatu Rijal, Seven Men, of Marrakesh. This custodian kept a stableful of young infidels who, he thought, were being drawn to Islam. They were all, of course, Germans who cared only for the free lodging. Their rucksacks and "mopeds" leaned against the courtyard wall. The old Muslim seemed not to mind leaving his unveiled wife and daughter in the house with a bunch of foreigners who were all but naked—the Germans, when they were not away sight-seeing, lounged in swimming trunks. I sat on the ground drinking tea with the wife and daughter and watching them make bread, which they then carried on their heads to the baker. They slept in the courtyards; the Germans and I were on the flagstones of a room with, in one corner, a twenty-five-foot well from which firebrats issued over the walls. Dysentery had made me quite weak, and the Germans, talking interminably, would not let me sleep. I had forgotten so much of their language that I did not think I could shut them up politely. At last, when everyone but me was asleep, there was a knock on the street gate. I went to answer it. To rouse me thoroughly, the light switch gave me a shock. The knocks were repeated; I called out *"Shkun!"* as I had heard the wife call when she went to open the gate, though I wasn't sure what it meant. There was a man with a basket of clothes.

He came in and woke the wife. I groped after sleep again. I counted my heartbeats; gradually I began to count wrongly, but I remember getting to four thousand. Curiosity led me to the back of the house, and in a room full of laundry I saw the basket-man and the wife, standing, but one or the other was upside down—I shall have to remember which, before I can annotate *The Perfumed Garden*.

Before leaving Marrakesh, I went back to the Jemaa el-Fna with a party of friends who had given me a robe and a pair of local sandals—that was all. I watched them for a time: six of them simply walked around, all speaking at once and holding out their hands for coins; one was dressed as a white-faced clown in harlequin suit, one carried a baby as if it were a doll and finally returned it to a group of women and children, and the band, sitting in the edge of the crowd, played a fast piece with a strong beat, led by an old man who blew an eight-holed pipe with more force than clarity. Then I went to work as they advised. I watched tourists till one took a photo of me (since I towered over the crowd, any panorama included me), and then I walked purposefully up to him and in a broken accent demanded money for having my face carried off. I wish I could say I had been a storyteller in the Jemaa el-Fna; I had memories enough and imagination enough, but not enough language. As a matter of fact, the spectacles that drew the largest crowds were frenzied arguments, and I wondered whether these were staged. But I left with enough money to walk back through Morocco without drawing, or even seeing, another face, except to buy melons and bread.

I must have been almost entirely composed of water. I drank from every stream and irrigation channel I crossed, if it was in hills where only storks might use it between me and its source. Perhaps I was lucky to be dried out by the Tadla, a great dust bowl in the middle of Morocco, surrounded by higher land that cut it off from rain and cooling breezes. The water in it is saline. In the country after it, the colors seemed rich, bright green to flaming red, as if blood was returning to the face of a man who had fainted in the heat of the Tadla.

A glimpse of a farmer and his girl standing in an orchard, kissing. A beautiful glimpse in evening afterglow, though the pose was learned from a film—Arabs and Berbers do not kiss.

I slowed my stride to accompany a troop of Arabs and donkeys. One donkey had a whole live sheep in one pannier and nothing in the other to balance it. Every so often a donkey would fall and take a rest; its master would shout, *"Arraazi! Rrrr!"* in vain indignation till the donkey chose to get up—when the panniers, having a strap at the back only, would come off. A smart car stopped, and the Arabs prepared to wave in protest at the photographer; but the man shouted at me, "Get your beasts off the road! Oh, you're French. Climb in." Accustomed to instant acceptance of offers, I climbed in before reflecting that I preferred the former company. This Frenchman, owner of an orange *domaine* near Tarudant, was going to visit his wife and daughter on holiday in one of the ski resorts of the Middle Atlas. *"We* never allowed the Moors to drive their animals on the roads," he said. "The only roads they keep in repair now are a few strategic ones, at American insistence. . . . You may think the Arabs here a stupid and dirty lot, but they're good compared with the Syrians. They work well when directed. . . . Bars aren't allowed to serve Muslims—so they have no resistance to alcohol. The brutalities at Meknes were started by men who preached holy war and then passed out the drink. . . . They've got trade unions here now. But *my* workers, when they were told to work a nine-hour day, they insisted on working a tenth hour if I gave them a bit of hay for their animals. . . . Berbers are a bit better than Arabs. . . . See those pipelines? They come from one of the biggest water projects in the world. The cost to France was terrific. . . ." I was resolving to cuckold this man. It's the only way I ever attack people.

The green poplar-adorned hollow with Azru at its far end opened under us. Then the second resort, Ifran, in what might have been English wooded downland, but that the soil was red and didn't hide all the rocks. There was even a ring of Girl Guides dancing in a meadow. Then Immuzer and a hired chalet on a grassy hillside. Doing the daughter's portrait, I walked to her and touched her. She blushed, locked the door, and stepped out of her clothes before the blush had faded from the base of her spine. When I was sure I had pleased her, I said to her: "Resist your father and be like me in one way: don't despise the native people."

All the sophisticates of the cities were here for the hot season, but I did not care to stay and do more fancy portraits. I revisited my humbler friends in Fez and Meknes. A Corsican engineering superintendent for the little towns round about Meknes took me out with him each day to build drains in el-Hajeb, Taujdat, and then Mulay Idris. I had seen no steep mountain-clinging Arab city before Mulay Idris. It was the engineer's despair, because to preserve its appearance each house that fell had to be rebuilt exactly as it had been—and they fell frequently, having no foundations. A wooden bar across the end of a broad white passage kept non-Muslims from the heart of the sacred city, but I went up a roofed staircase doubling back to the side, then a long succession of stepped streets, under arches, through mire and over bare rock, past tunnels leading to private houses, till I came to the topmost point, and stepped out onto a roof to paint a hurried picture. The countryside was now damp from rain (crape myrtles and paper flowers postponed their rustling) and for a change it was pleasanter to walk in the sun than the shade. I entered the ruins of Volubilis at night to avoid paying fifty francs, and made my bed in a disused stork's nest on one of the door lintels of the basilica. I approached at sunset the ridge before Petitjean: the red light came through the gorge and made it alone luminous while the rest of the ridge was black.

I came back to Tangier by side roads that led up steep little valleys behind the town onto a ridge, bounded on the other side by cliffs, the straits, and the view of Spain. On top here were a British hospital and compound. As I walked away, a hearty voice said, "Hello! I see a broad British back!" A missionary had mistaken me for someone he was expecting. So I stayed in a rest home for Anglo-Saxon holy men from all over Morocco. I slept in a classroom with cats, one within each bend of my body, so that I was compelled to stay still and got to sleep in under an hour. There was a view down on a stadium where on Crown Prince Mulay Hassan's birthday there were horse races, won by himself. I joined in the making of waffles with a machine just proudly bought from the American base at Sidi Sliman; I spent evenings playing Scrabble (the only vice of missionaries); I was taken through the hospital wards, shaking hands with the patients, and then told to wash my hands, since they had tuberculosis.

The lady missionaries had adopted an Arab girl and brought her up to be European in every way. But there is no legal adoption of Moroccans by Europeans. So nothing prevented her father (a backsliding Christian convert) from marrying her off, perhaps to some ignorant old tyrant, the moment he needed money. And in fact he had now given notice that he wanted to do so. The law had just been changed a little: the minimum age for marriage was raised, and instead of only the bridegroom signing the contract, the bride had to sign it too, thus getting a few moments in which to see him and refuse. Hind was just coming up to the minimum age.

I wanted to ask the missionaries why they did not take her out of the country—to Gibraltar or to England, where alone she was now fitted to live. But as I thought of asking my question, I realized that even to ask it was impossible. These upright people would not deceive her father, let alone get the false papers that would be necessary. They suffered small martyrdoms for their alien principles. One of them who lived in Tetuan regularly traveled all round by way of Wezzan because a certain official had once asked him for a bribe at a customs post. They also suffered inwardly from their own view of the Arabs. One said, "The Chinese have *some* good points but the Arabs have none. There's nothing beautiful about this people. It is for me a terrible temptation to despise them, but I am forbidden to do so."

". . . nothing beautiful about this people." I met Hind. I went down to the medina and by the sea, hoping in some way to make contact again with Ri and Milcíades, my smuggling friends. I got a stony reception in the café where I enquired. Failing them, there must be someone in this notorious free port who could arrange the transit of a girl across the straits. I had some hope with a Yugo-slavian who had been eight years in the Foreign Legion in Algeria and had retired to use his harder skills here. But seeing him drunk ruled him out. I found two people talking in a strange language and behaving furtively; I hopefully kept close to them till I found they were speaking pig Latin ("Oursay lipsay siay howingsay" for "Your slip is showing") so that sharp Moors wouldn't know they were American and overcharge them. A boy in a white woollen cloak showed me his school report from the *medersa*, and in the middle he had stuck a proposition and a list of names. Another boy took me to a beach hut that had been rented by an Italian couple; the gang had prepared a chink for viewing and were making money fast, for the Italian liked to spring on her still wet after every bathe. A man offered me a diamond ring for a thousand pesetas. Said he had "found" it on the beach, and scratched lines with it on a shop window to prove it was diamond. After I had shaken him off I wondered whether perhaps it *was* diamond. When next a man sidled up to me with a ring, I was receptive. Of course I couldn't buy a ring, but I wanted any contact with shady dealers. He was holding the ring low to his loins, and shielding it from other eyes with the corners of his jacket. Then I followed him to the beach. He met a group of men, all Spanish, as I could tell by their shoes (Spanish shoeblacks should be called either cigarette sellers, since that is most of their trade, or shoe whites, since the white upper is most of the shoe). They pointed out to sea. They offered me a swimming costume. I declined, remembering the Mowei-lihi ladies. They wanted me to swim out to a lido with a mass of people on it. I swam in my clothes, having nothing to lose. I climbed aboard into an orgy—a disappointing one, with no women. I had misunderstood the meaning of the second ring.

And so I strove to get embroiled with the underworld, between meals and services with the missionaries.

At last my mind noticed something my eyes had been staring at: a picture by myself, on a wall in the mission. I asked where it had been acquired, and they said from an agent called Afrodisio Escrántravel, or Descuelpte, or something like that. He would no doubt be back selling something in a day or two. He came (he was Milcíades, of course) with a donkey-load of plastic pails. (Water was cut off in Tangier except for three hours in the afternoon, when everybody filled baths and as many pails as they had.) I took Milcíades, Hind, and Hind's brother to the Moorish café on, or level with, the north wall of the casbah. Our discussion was accompanied by violin, tambourine, lute, a small high drum, and a song in which Hind's brother joined. Milcíades asked what he would get for making the arrangements. I said, "You can have the money you got for my basket, tent, clothes, and pictures." "I have it already," he said without blushing. I swallowed and offered him the asset worth more than money—my passport. He had to have it now, in case he needed it in the operation. After all, was it more important for her to get across the straits or me? I would survive anyhow. He told me to be in Gibraltar in a week's time. He sent me with a footballer called Allal (short for Abdalali) Allaly, who, as often happens, had been picked by Spanish talent scouts. Allaly and I went by paths to Tetuan (where we slept in a railway station built for a railway that was never built) and Ceuta, still part of Spain. In the morning, when Gibraltar was two inclined pinnacles riding above the mist, we posed as porters and carried my basket through a hole in the side of the *Virgen de África*. From Algeciras I walked round the bay, took my basket to the best wasteland hiding place I could find, and then, with only coins and a razor in my pockets, waded out at night east from La Línea and went south with the current. I didn't know the current turned outward as it met the tide from the Atlantic, but it wasn't too strong and I got ashore. With daylight, I had a fine secluded suntrap in which to dry off: a huge concrete catchment area for rain, on the eastward precipice of Gibraltar. On succeeding days I slept in the Alameda Gardens and in military areas, where I was undisturbed except by Barbary apes, and walked about at night, because there was now a Levant wind and everything was wet from the grey cloud sitting on the Rock. I found no warmth except in the shops of Indians, who stayed open all hours and were content to just talk. At last one morning a "ss!" sounded clear across a harbor. I walked round and met a man who said, "Milcíades is in prison. He told me to tell you he couldn't deliver your—" and the last word was *anadeja*. I wondered what it meant, but had other thoughts besides philology.

I got out of Gibraltar with the co-operation of a couple who had a season ticket for a beach just before Estepona, enabling them to avoid formalities at the frontier. My basket had been discovered by peasants, who kindly put up a cane-matting sun shelter beside it for me. Throughout Spain I now had to be ready to disappear whenever I caught sight of the state police, who walked around asking everyone's business. They were distinguishable from the municipal police by their grey-green uniforms and shiny black hats with flat backs, said to be designed so the policeman can go to sleep while standing against a wall. The only time I came in range of one was when he stopped

/ 171

a British car for not sounding its horn at a corner. *"Pi-pi obligatorio!"* said the policeman in basic Spanish, but the foreigner showed that he still misunderstood, and the policeman looked wildly round for an interpreter.

I went by way of Málaga, Granada, Motril. At Almería there was a *feria*, and I sold pictures of the families arriving at the bullfight in their costumes and coaches. In a moonlit rusty-and-grey desert of rocks (often daubed with *Franco Franco Franco* or *Arriba España* or *Todo Por La Patria* or *Mejores No Hay*—only, that last was an ad for Phillips's rubber soles) the only soft places were little patches of heather, but they were full of mosquitoes, so I slept on the shingly beds of dry rivers. Once I found something better, a clean concrete irrigation channel evidently not in use. It was turned on just before dawn; I was awakened by a distant rustle, then water shot over me, and was temporarily dammed by my basket, which blocked the channel just beyond me, thus building up extra inches over my face as I struggled out of my blankets. It was easy to live off the country at this season. Pomegranates overhung the road.

I arrived in the Grao of Valencia and walked along to the ticket office for the ship to the Baleares just as it closed, but I wanted to go, so I went out along the quay, boarded the *Rey Jaime II*, and asked if I could buy a ticket on board. This being irregular, and the captain being ill in bed, I was told to wait till the First Officer came. So I waited on board, while all the paying passengers stood in a mass on the quay. When they came up the gangplank, I moved with them into the interior of the ship. I slept at the bow, with two gypsy couples. Deck-class passengers were complaining about what they called the pigsty conditions, but to me the fly-free salt-softened boards were luxurious. It rained.

Mallorca was occupied by fat Englishwomen, smearing themselves with sun lotion. Trying to get away from them, I went in a boat along the rocky coast from Soller to the inlet of La Calobra, and through the tunnel to the beach at the neighboring inlet of the Torrent de Pareis— and was still amid fat Englishwomen. They stepped over the oil-smeared bank of shingle, but patches of oil floated in the water. When they came out, the beach attendant was ready behind a table to sell them petrol for cleaning themselves. I saved several people from him by rubbing them with gravel, the way I clean everything. One was a Dutchman whose father managed the Aerotour office in the Borne (officially, Calle del Generalísimo Franco). The father gave us free places on coach excursions. One day we went to Valldemosa, shuffled in slow columns through the monastery, and were entertained by dancers who were absolutely unsmiling, because as soon as we filed out the next coach-load would file in. Another time we went to Manacor and were part of the two thousand a day guided round the caves.

I usually have one book with me, and now it was Robert Graves's *Greek Myths*. Someone gave me it in Gibraltar, and I used the short stories in it for English lessons to Spaniards. I wished that Demeter would give to me, as to Pandareus, "the royal gift of never having the belly-ache"; and I stopped reading when I came to the man who was punished by the gods with perpetual hunger, so that his family turned him out and he ate dirt. On the back cover it said that Graves lived in Deyá, Mallorca. So I visited him. When he asked me why, I said that his book was my whole library (it had two volumes) and also that I once offered some poems to a publisher, who replied that he only published poems by Robert Graves.

People arriving in Mallorca found they couldn't get on a ship back for many days. So I bought a ticket for a Wednesday, and when Wednesday came I sold it at increased price to someone who otherwise couldn't have gone home till Friday. For my own return journey I walked on board again and tried my luck with another irregular request: that I might pay at the other end. Again I was told to wait for the First Officer. But this time I couldn't merge into the ship before he came. I explained to him that I had to hurry and it was too late to change traveler's cheques (which I didn't have). An Indonesian gentleman, overhearing, offered me a loan. I courteously declined, and all this caused the First Officer so much hesitation that by now the ship was in motion. The poor Indonesian, though he had to travel thousands of miles by sea, always got seasick and therefore went first class so as to be ill in private. As I was ill too, he didn't mind having me there. For someone with neither passport nor ticket nor shoes, I made myself rather rashly at home in the first-class quarters. I had half shaved my face in the bathroom when a waiter came and ordered me out. I said it was the only bathroom in the ship, but he stood with back turned and arms folded, so I turned my back too and finished shaving. We called at Ibiza, and as we left it the waiter came up to me and said, "Why didn't you change your money there?" "It's Sunday," I said, but he turned his back in the same irritating way, and I had a frightening urge to knock him overboard. I went to my friend's cabin to ask for the loan after all, and walked in on a lady—my friend had got off at Ibiza. The lady became my friend instead. She reported that the First Officer had just marched into the restaurant with a posse of sailors to take my passport from me, so I stayed in the cabin. The door wouldn't lock, and she soaped the knob so no one could turn it. I had a better idea: happening to have a pine cone, I smeared the knob with resin, and when we observed a steward scrubbing his hand for half an hour, we knew he was guilty. At Alicante I waited on the ship till the next lot of passengers was coming on board, then went down the gangplank against the stream as if I was one of them who had forgotten something. I met some boys who had stolen a lot of traveler's cheques from homosexuals on the beach, and they wanted me to cash some British ones: when the clerk at the bank asked to see my passport, I could explain that the captain of the ship had it and that I couldn't get it back till I had the money. I wasn't sure how traveler's cheques worked, but I thought the original owner might still save his money if nobody cashed them; so I decided to take the cheques and tear them up. But I could not get out of the bank without the boys seeing me, and to avoid being beaten up I had to walk round in public places till they tired of following.

Still using these experiences for suggestions, I took the chance to stay in a *pensión* and do some washing, because I could give a reason for temporarily having no passport. So the proprietor didn't fill in the usual police forms, for which there is an extra tax. He was an an old man who slept at night in an armchair in his office.

North slowly via Valencia again, Sagunto, and the plain densely covered with orange trees. At Castellón de la Plana I bought my first footwear, a pair of peasant rope-soled shoes for twenty-five pesetas, to put on when custodians of churches and other buildings wouldn't let me in barefooted. I found two old ladies picking flowers by the roadside; they had stopped their car to give me a ride, and I couldn't refuse. I accepted another ride on a cart carrying a huge load of palm leaves. And almost every scooter that passed me in Spain offered me a ride; I accepted once, but the cold and the ache through being pulled backward by my basket slung over my shoulder were almost unbearable. Just walking was best to stave off the pangs of my illness. Tarragona, I think, marked the stage where I became unable to enjoy seeing a new place. I noticed I could not spare the footsteps for walking round the Paseo Arqueológico on the city ramparts. I saved every step for my direct march to San Sebastián, nearest point to England before the border. Blue clouds and thunderstorms followed me along the hills fringing the Ebro. Cities were now places to get through quickly in case the diarrhea came on. And one day I realized I was walking without my basket. In my dreaminess, I did not know where I had left it. I had lost my paintings all over again, and the things to keep me warm at night. Thinner even than usual, I could not survive nights in the wet green mountains of Navarre. I tried to find a hostel in Pamplona, and the experience shows why animals and I avoid buildings when we are fit. Late at night, I was before a large dark modern educational building. I pressed on the bell push for some minutes. A woman appeared on high and told me to go into another street and turn right and look on my left. There I found apartments. I knocked on a lighted window, and a man directed me back where I had come from. I begged him to come to the window and point to the exact building, but he could not because he was in bed with his wife. I went back and pressed more minutes on the same bell push. A crowd of young women came out on a balcony. Noticing a tearful note in my voice, they did not lose patience, but directed me to the same place as before. In another street I saw a light in a garage and found a man repairing a car. He gave me a fresh direction, which led to where the street faded into wasteland. I tried turning left where he said right, and was in the midst of more educational buildings of uncertain purpose—empty but impregnable concrete castles towering into the dark. I burrowed into a load of hay on a truck, and only just managed to get clear when the driver got into it and drove off. I met a policeman around dawn, and asked him to show me a *casa de huéspedes* ("Cheaper than a *pensión,* but fit only for Spaniards," someone had told me). The policeman rapped on a door and brought an old woman down. She took me up three stories to a little windowless room where someone else was asleep. The stuffiness gave me a burning thirst, but the only water was some dregs in a bucket. I drank it, and immediately lost all I had ever eaten and more besides. The other man switched the light on, and it was at this point that I caught sight of myself in a mirror. My cheeks and temples were *not there.* I realized I might die. (And all for not yet knowing the simple remedy: take nothing for twenty-four hours except dry stale bread and neat tea.)

I determined to catch the train, and to get some food inside me. At the bar of the station *fonda* I bought the staple food of Spain, *um bocadillo de pan,* with a slice of meat in it, but made the mistake of getting a bottle of red wine (cheaper than lemonade) to wash it down. Of course in five minutes I was dead drunk. I and the almost full bottle lay down side by side, and I seemed about to sleep when I turned over and painted the station floor with purple bread. The train was moving out; I jumped for the open platform on the end of the last carriage, and would certainly have fallen back if people had not pulled me on. In San Sebastián I told the British vice-consul I had lost my passport. I remembered the number, date of renewal, and even —after a moment of difficulty—name. He would get me an emergency visa, but it would have to be approved by local authorities tomorrow. "You seem to have jaundice or sprue," he said, and gave me a bottle of angostura, telling me to soak cubes of sugar with it and suck them. I consumed the day by drinking *gaseosa* (cheaper than wine) and then a siphon of soda (cheaper than *gaseosa*) to take the taste of the angostura away, and absorb my saliva, and keep me a place at a table. A lady gave me much crushed banana, and this seemed to begin my cure. The rest of my troubles before I left this place loomed large, as does an itch in the middle of the night, but faded beside the troubles of others. There was a Norwegian couple who, with the wife's mother, had been staying in France, and had bribed an official to let them cross the border to San Sebastián for a day without visas. The old lady had a weak heart, got sunstroke, and died. They could not report her death because they were in Spain illegally, so they wrapped her in a rug, put her in the luggage compartment, and drove back to the border. While they were bribing the officials again, the car was stolen, with the corpse in it. They couldn't report that either. Back in Norway, with no death certificate, they are unable even to wind up the old lady's large estate.

I paid for a *couchette* on the train all the way to Paris. From each doze I was awakened by saliva forming a pool on the leather. I was sent to the Hospital for Tropical Diseases in London. I tried to escape, feeling that all I needed was someone to mother me. They found I weighed seven stone (ninety-eight pounds). The corners of my mouth were drawn back in an unfelt grin, and when I was put in a bath my backbone tapped the enamel like a row of knuckles. The nurses made me give them a full narrative of how I had got like this, an installment an evening. It was an ordeal, because they kept finding fault with my ability to look after myself. They came past the ends of the beds at night, waking me by tapping my feet, which stuck out into the aisle against regulations.

Some of these nurses intended to join the Aldermaston March. Listening to the argument—is violence ever permissible?; sometimes violence is necessary; violence is the only way—I bit the safety catch from a grenade and tossed it among them. I thought that after they had felt the proximity of violence, in blood vessels, in adrenalin, they would be qualified to say, "Violence is sometimes necessary." It was a pine cone I still had. They were girls, they didn't know a grenade when they saw one, my pine cone fell flat.

Here, while I was being fed like a baby on milk, my pictures lost in Zaragoza were amazingly sent back to me, though nothing else. When I got out, I was unready for the climate. I took shelter in a library, and opened a Spanish dictionary—*anadeja*, "duckling" . . .

. . . I found Levi's small enough in the
waist. Threw other trousers away. Later I
washed my Levi's in the Black Sea. They
shrank and even I couldn't get back into
them . . .

. . . at the end of a two-mile driveway at Seal
Chart in Kent, the cottage of Alban Hills,
editor of the *Hardware Trade Journal*. This
being run by Benn Bros., who also publish the
Blue Guides, visiting him were Blue Guides
editor L. Russell Muirhead and his assistant
editor, Joan Hitchcocks, who called him Telly.
There are only three on the permanent staff
and they never go abroad. I said I had used
a Guide Bleu in some country and liked the
travel language. *Collines qu'enlace la route
—un étranglement de la valée—
—piste pour les chameaux—défilé exigu
qu'elle franchit en corniche.* Said Telly, "We
have no connection with Guides Bleus—we
only look like them" . .

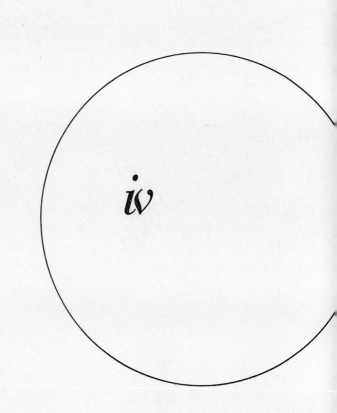

iv

Go, vagabond, flit, vagabond, wander, never met
you, we forget, vagabond man!

Sag, wagabond, nag, lagabond, languor, aye and
anger and ire, eh, dragabond man?

Long are you strong, wrong, are you strong, ponder?
to the end, then, not a friend, ragabond man!

. . . man called C. J. Cield gave me his
notebook with a stiff cover marked HARDWARE
TRADES FEDERATION CONFERENCE MATLOCK
1959 / SUPER "BLUEBELL" BALER TWINE
"BLUEBELL" BINDER TWINE. Told me to keep
it in a hip pocket so every time I sat down I'd
remember to write something in it. I never
began . . .

. . . May in south Britain: moles killed all
over the roads. May in north Britain: Scots
pine pollen heaped along the margins of
ponds . . .

flitting

On the northern side of Manchester there is a piece of land called Boggart's Hole Clough. The story is of a house that once stood there and was haunted by a boggart, a bad spirit. At length the man who lived in the house had had his bellyful of the boggart and decided to leave. He spent a week packing his trunks, and was loading them on the dray when a neighbor came past.

"What, John," said the neighbor, "are ye flitting?"

"Yes, neighbor, we're all flitting," piped a little voice from inside one of the trunks.

So John saw he might as well stay put.

In a snack bar I fell into conversation with a man in a raincoat. He told me about his job, which was, he said, bomb disposal. As soon as he took his departure, another man in a raincoat approached and stood over me.

"Did I hear that your name is Walker?" he said.

I looked at him blankly.

"Perhaps he said I'm a great walker," I suggested.

"You haven't just bought a house?"

"No, I haven't just bought a house."

The man looked around, then pulled a chair out and sat down with me.

"Something sinister is happening," he said. "I have moved house four times in the last six years. *And every time, the name of the people who moved into the house that I moved out of was*—you know what it was?"

"No," I said. (I am slow-brained.)

"*Walker.*

"Yes. I have a shrewd suspicion, all right. Walkers are taking over this country solid. . . ."

. . . the tiredest I ever got, I saw the man
who lay down beside me go to sleep and turn
into a baby. Terrified, I woke him, and he
turned back into a man . . .

. . . under bushes in a city park. In the
morning a man cycled through. He dismounted
at the edge of a pond, laid himself carefully
in the water on his right side, then remounted
and cycled back the way he had come.
    I thought about it, and decided he didn't want
to go to work, and so pretended (to his wife)
that he had fallen into the pond on his
way . . .

. . . a drunk at a pub climbed on a table.
I murmured, "Hippocleides don't care." A
man with a twinge of grey hair, impressed by
my knowledge of the classics, took me home to
paint a mural across the end of a room: it was to
be anything that harmonized with the Greek
vases on the wallpaper of the other four walls.
I painted a life-size chariot. I hadn't stripped
and cleaned the wall and filled the cracks and
dents; probably it is now all gone . . .

. . . only umbrellas are much use against the
rain. I had one, but dropped it, because to
carry anything in one hand while pulling the
basket with the other caused backache . . .

. . . being asked how I could tell they were cows and not horses at such a distance set me thinking: the distinctive features of cows were their wall-like nostrils and wall-like pelvises; I flecked the distant hillside in the picture with the nostrils and pelvises—only—of cows. Nobody recognized them . . .

. . . everything seeming green as I came indoors, I picked up a sandwich and bit it. It wasn't a sandwich but a handkerchief Dominique had just ironed and folded triangularly.

I feared a spreading of the blind spot. I realized how much I needed my eyes. I thought of piercing my eardrums—blindness as well as deafness couldn't happen, not both of them . . .

. . . knocked. Distraught man opened the front door: "For God's sake, the last night before the removal men come and you want me to sit for my picture! Here, come in and help me." We worked till 4:00 A.M. at such tasks as cutting unused checks in half with a guillotine to make memorandum cards, and bashing a halfpenny with a knife handle (the hammer being packed) to make its crushed edge thinner so it could be used (the screw driver being packed) to unscrew bookshelves. Dusty, the man took a quick bath, called me to bring him the phone book, balanced it on his knees while checking the addresses of this-town people who had to stay on his Christmas-card list . . .

. . . excuses people give: "Only the little ones, and they're in bed"; "I'd have no one to leave it to"; "I've had me photo took that many times" . . . Sometimes on seeing my samples they turn and call, "Come and look, Julie—lovely photographs." Sometimes, when they pose, they first pass their tongues over their lips. They have been told to do this just before the photographer presses his trigger— it induces a natural look . . .

. . . worst times were when I took rests in towns, working as a laborer. Saved money by camping on the outskirts. Traveling out on the bus at evening; filthy rain, endless suburbs, closing year, sky even yellower through the bus windows, my weakness, ache in my shoulders. Had to get out, walk away from the lamplight, unroll my tent on a bomb site . . .

inside knowledge

Laboratories, beetling up to seven or eight stories, surrounded on three sides a row of old houses; the fourth side of the giant building was to be closed, so the little houses were being demolished. An old woman came with cigarettes for the wreckers, so they would let her take laths away for firewood.

There was great heat all week. I thought: "The world is more bad than good as long as people have to work other people's work all the sunlight hours. They should have most of them for leisure." But because I was not at a job myself, it was some time before I had a chance to say this to anybody. I said it to a park attendant, who replied, "Well, Bank Holiday's coming up."

The Bank Holiday weekend was THE GREATEST WASH-OUT EVER, said the newspaper, showing people under umbrellas on a sea front.

After the weekend, there was a bit of damage every two hundred yards or so: a park bench overturned, a railing pushed over, a litter basket squashed, a telephone gutted, the lid knocked off a floodlight cover. Young men's tiny efforts to dent an undentable world.

The thick old woman came shuffling along Denmark Road. She wore boots, two overcoats, and a thoroughly grey shawl that had once been an air-cell blanket. She paused to kick a brick off the asphalt into the gutter. A way of doing good: leaving the place one brick tidier. She turned into the park, and tried to set one of the overturned benches upright. Either, again, on the side of order, or wanting a bed. She was too weak, and I lifted it for her. I sat beside her on it for a short while.

We talked in a crazy way, and soon I felt I could offer a suggestion. "Why don't you wear the blue coat over the grey coat, instead of the other way round?"

"Eh?"

"Why don't you wear the blue coat over the grey coat, because the blue coat's longer? Then people won't see you've got two coats on."

She answered in a different voice, so intelligent that I thought a person half her age was speaking from inside her: "You live in a set of clothes for thirty years and you know the best way to wear it. I know the inside of my clothes so well—as well as if I'd got eyes all over me. I know there's a little hole now in the sole of my left boot, even though it's too small to see, because I feel it cold every time I step in the damp."

. . . on Ravenstonedale Common, when I got
to my feet at the moment of dawn after a
plum-purple night of rain, my shadow was cast
on the sky . . .

. . . three hours before sunrise, having slept
in a quarry above High Tilberthwaite, I came
along a mud road through the woods to a ford
over the river Brathay. The ford was an arc of
gravel facing upstream. A car had tried to go
straight across and was stuck in the middle.
I splashed past, noticed a man asleep inside.
A spider thread with a yellow leaf twizzling on
it connected the car with the trees
overhead . . .

. . . S.Q.G. was a Dutch missionary who had
railwayed round the world. I asked him to step
aside with me and see the parish church of
Tideswell, called the Cathedral of the Peak.
"What's so great about it?" "Well, if you walk
all the way round the inside of it touching the
wall, your finger will have traveled a mile."
He snapped, "If I wanted to wear my finger
out in any such stupid way I'd have put it on
the ground a year ago and it would have done
twenty-five thousand miles by now!" Anyway,
he came to see the church, and saying,
" 'Whosoever shall compel thee to go a mile,
go with him twain,' " he made us do a second
circuit . . .

. . . while Jo was talking she had both her front and her back doors open because it was hot. I was mentally painting her Conch (that is, Bahaman) face, and suddenly the room darkened and her face, being dark already, for a moment vanished. A storm was coming up outside . . .

. . . an agonized young man, Ron Blapp, who was himself doing a painting. It looked like an uncleaned palette (not a bad idea) but it was a vision: angels on the head of a pin and camels filing through the eye of a needle. A Discipline (instrument for mortification of the flesh) hung on his wall by a thong . . .

. . . farmer told me he believed cattle and stag beetles are succumbing to slowness and will die out like dinosaurs. Moreover, all his potatoes were attacked by dartrose . . .

. . . Sukie's brother gave me Cotton's *Geomorphology* so I could see the anatomy of the landscape. I said aloud the phrases I liked: "Wave-base. Resurrected drainage. Volcanic skeleton." Sukie, at this last: "Is that what you are?" Then, in a characteristic gesture, clapping hand over insucked lips to suppress wicked mirth . . .

. . . "When my husband comes in, keep quiet about the way you live. He's always saying he wishes he was a tramp. He's envious of me because I've married twice, so he hits at me by saying, 'If you don't look out, I'll go off and be a tramp.' I say to him, 'You silly old sod, you have to go to the dentist every second month, and you have to get new prescriptions for your glasses' " . . .

. . . prominent on a bathroom shelf was a little round bottle marked LOVE OIL. So at the appropriate moment I went to fetch it. Found it was really CLOVE OIL. She said, "It's for putting on the socket where I had my wisdom tooth extracted" . . .

red and green

The Sikhs came to Hulme on Wednesday, to Moss Side
(where their temple was) on Thursday. The lorry stopped
in a cross street, the sons jumped off and stalked along
parallel alleys, from their windpipes ripping a syllable
that seemed at first about to be:
    "Key!"—then:
    "Ken!"—then:
    "K.O.!"—then:
    "Kyaa-owl"—"Coal!"
Children followed imitating, and then yard gates opened
and housewives in carpet slippers, unshaven, their hair as
ghastly red as any Moroccan hennaed for a scalp disease,
showed themselves and gave their orders. The young men
hoisted the sacks with thin arms and balanced them against
their turbans. It was nearly Christmas. Yellow sitting
rooms burned within the heaps of black stone, yet it was
impossible to feel they were safe from the universal rain:
walls and flagstones, clad in shiny water, seemed already
in dissolution.

At a corner, the distressed face of a girl on her knees
turned up to me, and I asked if I could help. She said,
"I've gone and dropped my handkerchief through the slits
of this drain cover. I've been trying to get it up with these
twigs, but I can't."

I knelt too. The grating was partly rusted away, and the
gap was filled with a cat's cradle of wires from an electric
cord, in insulating plastic, some red and some green. We

couldn't untie the knots, slippery with rain. We tried to lift the whole grating, but it was stiff in its place with rust. "Do you actually need this particular handkerchief?" I asked. I thought it would be rather wet down there by now.

"It's got eucalyptus on it to clear my nose," she told me.

Rain streaming from our chins onto the backs of each other's hands, we probed the symbolic slits. It was like when the girl lays her hand on the milk-bar counter, two fingers making a V, and you stealthily slide one finger up between them—and if she notices but doesn't withdraw, you stroke the soft crotch between her knuckles.

"This isn't a drain cover," I said at last. "It's the chute to someone's coal hole."

We knocked at the door, and when it opened I said, "This young lady has dropped something into your coal cellar." "Come in, lass," said the housewife. I was left out in the rain, all for having said, "This young lady" instead of "My friend," or "We."

I walked on to the Fallowfield crossroads. I had been looking at the green lights as I came toward them. By squeezing my eyes narrow, I could turn traffic-light green (a white-blue-green) into a kind of yellow, even amber. I wondered why there were two green lights, side by side. Then one of them changed to amber, but the other did not, for it was not a traffic light, but a Christmas light hanging over the door of a shop. They had hung two lights there, shaped like bells, frozen in contrary swings. One was red and the other green. The mere colors have come to mean Christmas. Alas, the red light faced away from the crossroads, the green toward. Green, which says, "It's safe to go," is the color of danger—traffic lights green both ways. . . . A driver coming along the same street as me went straight over and hit two cars passing on the other street. I dragged him out and took him into the house of a dentist, who bandaged his foot, and away he went limping.

Rain clashing with the water on the ground leaped back into itself; the atmosphere seemed changing to water from the base up.

rag-bone

The rag-and-bone man came once a week with a nasalized
cry, "Raigbo!" He threw the reins over one shaft, gave the
horse some straw, and disappeared into the back alley,
where his position was flagged by the periodic "Ra-ig-bo!"
Or it could have been "Rag-mill." When he reappeared at
a corner, the horse rumbled forward to meet him.

At dusk I came across his cart, unattended in a lane
beside a playground. It was a bare platform with no walls,
two rubber wheels, and one shaft. I stopped and looked it
over, because it seemed small enough for me to pull, and
I could sleep on it.

Appleby bridge: I stood and waited above the saintly
river. I noticed the rag-and-bone man sitting cross-legged
on his cart on the quay. He was trying to mend a toy pistol
that someone had tossed onto his cart. The rag-and-bone
man had bleary eyes. Watching someone trying to mend
something is as bad as being tickled. I tried to do it for
him.

He coughed out a bolas of phlegm and said, "Waiting
for someone?"

"Yes."

"Who?"

"A woman," I said foolishly.

"Ah! That's nice. I'll stop and see her come, the
darling," said the rag-and-bone man.

I thought of offering him half a crown to go away. I was
afraid she would turn up, and wouldn't look good.

We could love the ones we are to love, regardless of looks, if we only had ourselves to consider. But we consider outsiders. We want to be sure they approve, or, rather, envy. There is too little secrecy, not too much. Secrecy should be absolute: nobody knows who makes love to whom, and nobody slyly reveals their luck either. That would be free love indeed. For you would love her because you love her, and not because you won't look over-ridiculous for it. You could even abstain from love in peace, for nobody would know.

. . . Mr. Glass, Cheshire art dealer: "Why do
you have to be so heterosexual? It's all very
fine, but why you? We should be able to predict
you by multiplying Open Road by Shopping
Basket by Portrait-Mongering, but you go and
add sex, which has nothing to do with it" . . .

. . . the Fylde: snow even on the beach. Tide
came in, cutting black arcs out of the
white . . .

. . . one black night I saw, at the edge of my
eye, a huge snake draw past me,
crackling with fire.
    It was the chain by which one truck towed
another. At the top of a rise the leading
truck changed gear, the other caught up, and
the chain dropped to fill itself with sparks
from the imprisoned gravel of the road.
Then the monster's captors yanked it up and
on, and the dark reconcealed its savagery . . .

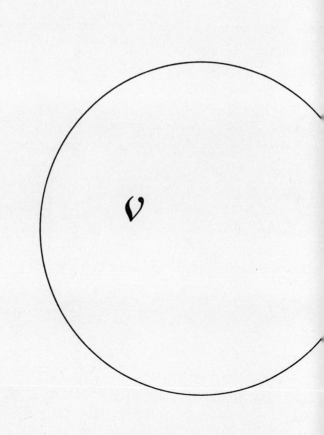

. . . a light changed, preventing us from getting to the Birkenhead front in time for the ferry. "Well," said a woman, "wouldn't that make you want to say your prayers backwards!" I asked her what she meant. She said people in Toronto, where she came from, said it at moments of sudden disappointment. "But does it mean you feel like going over to the devil and saying the Black Mass?" "I see you know a thing or two," she said, and gave me the address of a coven of witches I could join, led by Mrs. Sybil Leek, antique dealer, at Burley in Hampshire . . .

. . . two former British naval officers, one back in England and one in California. Each told me about a pleasure trip at the end of the war, when volunteers were asked to sail a score of yachts, lent by the Americans, back to their home ports via Grenada, Martinique, Key West. Each said he was the only one that volunteered; the rest had to be ordered; were unwilling to go out of reach of home for a month or two . . .

organdale

A lane near Bishop Auckland in County Durham. A storm, a lesser and a greater stroke of lightning, and I found myself walking back the way I had come, passing on my left the oaks and rowans I had seen on my right. And so I let myself be switched south.

Tourcoing. My eye, bobbing as I walked, caught a flapping of light in front of me, and thinking "Glass is a liquid" I walked so as to keep it in sight. It was from white and blue neon strips somewhere behind me, and it was reflected in glass which proved to be the far end of a bus shelter. Thus I found myself walking through the bus shelter, to the exit, where a bus presented its boarding platform, and I had to board. It took me back the way I had come, and so into the northward swing.

A car stopped by me and the driver asked, "Am I on the right road for Kendal?" I said no, she must go back to the main highway and then right. She drove ahead to find somewhere in the lane to turn round. Meanwhile suddenly I wanted to go south. Kendal was halfway to Lancaster. Lancaster was halfway to Manchester. . . . When the little car came back I waved and she stopped, thinking I had some more to inform her of.

Snakes-and-ladders; a fast southward snake. The manors, the copses, the bridges of months past reviewed in hours.

Fréjus. Going out through a suburb about dawn, I noticed a thread running along the base of the wall beside me. I followed it round a corner, round another. Round three sides of the block. Nobody was at the end of it, measuring; it was tied to the bole of a cade juniper. Facing now north, I began the summer's lap.

A seasonal migrant travels a shorter distance each year than those who stay in one locality, because a seasonal migrant moves toward the part of the earth that is leaning nearer to the sun.

You need a nonchalance about walking into cul-de-sacs, whether under the eyes of urchins in Marrakesh or vigilantes in Bel Air. No use trying to look as if you know where you're going. Look as if you don't *care* where you're going, which is the truth.

If I forget something I don't go back for it. Someone will almost at once resee me and ask if I am lost. Can't retrace more than a dozen steps before the bondage of being recognized begins.

Wind, so dominant that the land seems rushing northward and the leaves and newspapers getting left behind.

Why should I walk all day into such wind when I can walk with it?

Sometimes I was literally blown about by the wind, my daily transposition fixed by the wind's set and the number of hours I had nothing to do but walk. The only surprise was that I should come up in the same narrow funnel of England, instead of some other longitude, America, or Siberia.

Bernhardt Münch, on the carpet of whose hotel room I had slept, had a brochure on the "Phestibal Athenon." The concerts were to be in the Odeon of Herodes Atticus. I climbed in by a path along the floodlit flank of the Acropolis, and shared a stone seat with a gentleman called Jørgen Thordrup. He was an Anthroposophist. Afterward we discussed this occult system from midnight till dawn, not exactly in the Agora, but in a café on Omonias Square. He was on holiday from an Anthroposophical teacher-training school. He would be back at it in the spring and suggested I lay my route that way. It was at Dornach in Switzerland.

Some months later I was not thinking of this when I came through snow-covered fields to an upland village called Gempen. From the end of the ridge I saw into the valley of Liestal; at another point, a view over the valley of the Birs, from its quitting its gorge at Aesch to its joining the Rhine at Basel. Descending a track through woods, I passed among the snowdrifts a stump with a shield and pike set in it, commemorating a battle in 1499. This battle (at which the Swiss won the Swabian War and their independence from the Holy Roman Emperor) was the Battle of Dornach.

A crag called Gempenfluh projects from the horizon behind Dornach; after its profile Rudolf Steiner, founder of Anthroposophy, designed his Goetheanum. It is a huge mound of grey concrete, without any right angles. Inside there are some shrines and theaters. There is a cave where rest cremated Anthroposophists; over that, a concrete grotto housing the gigantic statue of Christ repelling Lucifer and Ahriman, which Steiner was finishing on the day of his death; higher, the Grundsteinsaal, "foundation-stone room," as the lesser theater is called; and over that, the great theater. Indeed, its stage is the second largest in Europe (the only larger being that of the Bolshoi in Moscow). Machinery and storage occupy still vaster volumes around it. It is used for eurhythmy and cloudy spiritual dramas.

Jørgen took me to lunch with Publio from Trieste, who was assistant stage manager. Publio told me I could work as a stagehand if I wished. He said many come to do that while making up their minds about Anthroposophy.

So I became a *Bühnenhilfer*. (Less formally, *Kulissenschieber*—"flat-shover.")

I had to learn German fast to understand not only my instructions, but also the patter of Harri Emmelot, a Dutchman among the stagehands, and a world-class comedian.

I remarked to Herr Jürgens that Emmelot could soon put Danny Kaye out of business.

"Actually, he was a professional actor once," Herr Jürgens told me, "but now he roams round Europe and can't get a job."

"Why?"

"Because they think he collaborated with the Nazis."

"And did he?"

"I don't suppose so; I suppose he was just trying to earn his bread."

But it was easy to see Emmelot in the role—his harsh Nordic head, stook of blond hair, which made him taller even than me, his leather britches and boots.

Besides Emmelot there were two other Dutchmen; one was the painter Logtenberg, and the other was Deckers or Dekkers. Dekkers contrasted with Emmelot—short, fat, dark, dimwitted.

In the middle of the *Tagung*, there were several days free, and Emmelot and Dekkers went for a tour into Italy on Emmelot's motorcycle. When they reached the St. Gotthard Pass and stopped to buy a drink, it came out that Dekkers had brought no money. So Emmelot left him there, and toured Italy alone. Arriving back first, he confessed he didn't know where Dekkers was. It took Dekkers four days to walk to Dornach, and on the way his shifty appearance and poor German got him taken in by the police.

When I left, it was because I had met Maarjalein (who was going to be a nurse in a Barnardo's home in Essex) and Ranftl (who was going to be a chef at a hotel in Torquay), and they had found a way to get a passage on one of the great barges of the Rhine. They take half as long from Basel down to Rotterdam as they do from Rotterdam up again to Basel.

Ferry from Sweden to Denmark. Waves poured through the Strait of Øresund from the North Sea; spray drove everyone from the deck. In Copenhagen it was not difficult to find the Rudolf Steiner school, though here it was called Vidarskolen after a Norse god of interest to Anthroposophists.

Jørgen had become a vegetarian, and took me for vegetarian meals to a lady called Fru Schou. Her apartment served as a resthouse for foreigners in the city, and I slept on the floor of the dining room. I was awakened by a young Faeroese in a dressing gown stepping to and fro across my head. Her name was Gyrithe, and with her I traveled to Lolland and then to Germany.

We were given a ride by a German chemist with a cataract in his eye and a way of rolling his head. We reached Gedser in time for the 1:30 ferry to Grossenbrode, but our driver only had a ticket for the 2:30. I chose to go ahead; Gyrithe chose to wait because the driver said he was going all the way to Oldenburg. So we separated, but it turned out he meant not the great Oldenburg-in-Oldenburg, but a little Oldenburg-in-Holstein just a few miles on, and so we met again. Later, receiving a letter from Gyrithe, I came back and returned with her from Hamburg to Copenhagen. The first time, the ferry had gone from Gedser to Grossenbrode (at a still earlier period it had been between Gedser and Wärnemünde); the second time, they had completed the Bird's-Flight Route: the ferry now from Grossenbrode to Rødbyhavn, and a road continuing the line of the three-kilometer Storstrømsbroen bridge, among the Danish islands. I remember wishing this way had been open the earlier year, for then the route of my migration from Helsinki to Hamburg would have made a still smoother curve on the map.

We stood in the sleet looking out at the island where Tycho Brahe lived, and at the ships passing through the Øresund. Traffic came in bursts from the ferries at Elsinore, and one of a pair of sailors was knocked down. We helped get him to a hospital. His friend said, "Our ship's leaving for the Persian Gulf at four o'clock." Then he told me I could probably join in the place of the injured man. But for Gyrithe I would have.

Instead we joined a man called Aagondael and helped him buy pianos. His forename, Aage, was pronounced like *augur*. Aagondael's trade was this: he traveled to Iceland with pianos and came back with sheepskins. For in Iceland they have a surplus of sheepskins but a dearth of pianos to play in the long arctic night.

The ship touched at Leith and at the Faeroes, where it lost Gyrithe.

I told the authorities I planned to interview modern Icelandic poets.

They said, "Yes, we had another like you. Next thing he was interviewing modern Icelandic businessmen, and in the end we found him interviewing modern Icelandic Communists."

The roads in Iceland are lacerated by the winter, and in the short summer they pay you a lot to work repairing them. But you can't take the money out of the country. So I was advised to take it out in the form of a tape recorder, a carpet, a set of nesting suitcases, and anything else I needed. But I didn't need anything.

In Reykjavik I found the Dutchman Dekkers. He had a summer job like me, though unlike me he spent all his earnings on beer. He viewed the approaching winter with glee, however, because it would bring his revenge on Emmelot.

"I vot wrote to Emmelot," he said. "I vot tell him, plenty of work here all year round, good money, good women. Emmelot vot come."

So Emmelot would arrive in the Iceland winter and find there was no work to be had at all.

Next time I saw Dekkers, he had received a letter from Emmelot, and "Emmelot vot certainly coming."

"The only trouble about my plan," Dekkers said, "Emmelot vot murder me."

A week and a half later, Dekkers said, "Emmelot vot be here soon. How I vot going to to get away? I vot not got any money."

Here was a use for my money. I split it, and Dekkers and I took ship for New York.

In New York I found Herr Jürgens. He had emigrated and had a job in Brooklyn. He said people called him Mister Joygens or just Joyg.

"How do I get across the Atlantic and back for nothing?" asked a graduate student in an English department.

I began to write down for him the address of Aagondael. "Isn't that the name of an archangel?" he said. Angels' names end with *el,* demons' names with *on,* he said.

I was taken to a party to be teased. "How did you come to be over here? Shouldn't you still be working from village to village? Wasn't it against your principles to go suddenly flipping across an ocean?"

Again I started explaining about Aagondael. Rock-and-roll caused someone to mishear and think the *Organdale* was a sort of Great Circle.

When I was a thousand miles from the Pacific and half as far again from the Atlantic, but half asleep, I seemed to hear a foghorn. It was an illusion—the wind blowing through the air-vent of a house—but it put in my mind again the misty groan of that word *Organdale,* along with the drift ice, the cake-shaped islands, the grey harmony of ships passing; the Road of Swans, the Vikings called it.

An Organdale is a natural route. It is a line that fits well to a map, seemingly grown there in some such way as the rivers, the fault lines, the frontiers of glaciation, the northern limit of palms. It is a regular curve, except as nudged by bays and mountains or refracted by the grain of the land. It exploits geologic weaknesses, as a volcanic sill does. It is a list of coasts, ferries, the margins of forests, and the influences of winds and shadows. It is a climbing along the arch of islands, not just straight over by plane.

My Organdale should have taken in the Orkneys, the Shetlands, Greenland, and Montreal. But steamship companies do not cognize Organdales. There is, for another example, no way from Sicily to Tunisia.

An Organdale is also a route marked out by human signposts. It is going next where the story slips to. People and winds both blow, and I do not resist.

Seas crossing search
By slumber loosed,
Spray angels perch
On Sumburgh Roost . . .

. . . I had planned to say, if ever I fetched
up at the border of the United States, "I am a
homosexual Communist Negro. Yes, a
homosexual Communist atheist illiterate
unemployed divorced Jewish Catholic Arab
Negro. Female. Left-handed. Red-haired.
Syphilitic. Of no fixed address. Intellectual.
Penniless. Motherless. With intent to set up a
bawdyhouse." I forgot to do so. . . .

. . . "Detectives are looking for a tall thin
man," said a radio in a workers' canteen
wagon as I passed, then traffic noises cut it
off . . .

. . . Jo got up from the grass, slapped
herself, opened her handbag, took out a roll
of sticky paper, tore off a strip, applied it to
her buttocks, removed it, applied it again.
    I: "What are you doing?"
    "Getting the dust off my clothes."
    "There's no dust on."
    "You! You're all dust. Stand still."
    She knelt and stropped me all over with bits
of sticky paper. They made strong kissing
noises . . .

. . . black shoeshine boy didn't see I had no
shoes, called, "Put 'em up here, sir." I
laughed and put my foot on his box. So he
laughed and went ahead and blacked it . . .

. . . I passed through a country gas station in the early morning. I had on my basket a wrecked harp, which I had picked out of a trash can, hoping to make it work. It was heavy enough to ring the bell as I passed over the cord, waking an angry attendant . . .

. . . at first in America I charged a simple dollar, like a simple pound in England. Began to notice I wasn't living so well . . .

. . . sat on my lap, wearing a green corduroy skirt. When she got up, there showed clearly on my thigh the outline (like a brass rubbing) of a key that was in my pocket. She wanted to know why should I have a key? What had I to unlock? A house somewhere? A car, bicycle, box of goods? Was it the key to someone else's house? . . .

. . . went to sleep while studying a windscape (or windscrape) of cirrus. I woke with a sharp pain. My navel was burning. The sun had heated the brass rivet at my waist . . .

. . . all the time they talked I could see one star out of the window, and at last I had to go out and see what it was. Alfard, "The Lonely." As I stepped back in I heard someone say, "He won't come back. What an excuse for leaving!" . . .

. . . they didn't invite me to stay, but I slipped back in to spend the night in a now-

disused tower room where the old man had
left a telescope. From here a trap door and a
sliding ladder led down to a landing,
approached only by a boxed-in servants'
stair, and on the landing was a piano.
I put my foot on the soft pedal and with one
cautious finger began verifying tunes I had
thought of in the past months. Feet sounded on
the stair. I hastily shut the lid of the keyboard,
but I hadn't noticed a music rest hinged to the
underside of the lid, a music rest of a type that
had to be folded up first. It smashed out a
chord of eighteen black notes . . .

. . . "The first night we moved in here, I
thought the roof had flown away—I thought we
were out in the open." I: "Why?" She turned
the bedroom light off. Transparent plastic stars
had been stuck to the ceiling, and they glowed
in the dark . . .

. . . "Paint faces, do you? Well, you can do a
disguise job on me. See this red rash on my
neck and these spots on the point of my chin?
I've got to go for an interview in a few minutes,
and I shaved myself too hard" . . .

. . . with Jallung the prospector into the hills
of Colorado. I carried his black-light box.
We saw a glint of the wild blue radiance of,
he told me, scheelite, the mineral containing
tungsten. I reached for it. A knife, it seemed,
went into me. Scheelite isn't the only thing that

glows light blue in ultraviolet light: so do
scorpions . . .

. . . traveling out to live in a subdivision in
the Mohave Desert, taking a flat of Dichondra
(that is, a box of it in earth), hoping to grow a
lawn from it . . .

. . . caught a ride with Barnum & Bailey's
circus train headed for Mexico. At one o'clock
in the night it halted at Indio. I got out under
an overhanging roof, from which (it seemed)
a wall of heat was descending, as in front of
some city stores in cold northern
Christmases. I asked somebody, "Why are the
heaters on?" "Heaters? That's the climate
here" . . .

. . . as I passed the end wall of an
architect's office there were hammer thuds,
then a chunk of the wall fell out at my feet.
"Making a door?" I said to the faces inside.
"No," they said, "trying to hang a picture" . . .

voice

I closed a door in Manchester behind me, and walked away among grimy midnight streets. I was trying to get through to the road out to the south. At last I came to a cavernous space or alley between high black buildings. At the farther end I could see the lights of the highroad, but the space, which was dark and which might have been silent, was filled with a somber sound—a sound that for a moment I took to be foghorns and fulmars of a rockbound sea. It was music—a French horn; they were rehearsing up behind the windows that studded the towering black side of a music school. Then from somewhere within the building a soprano sailed out on a high scream. She showered down through angled steps to a contralto sob which opened a whole Ireland in my soul. Behind her was the harmonic cushion of an organ. It was a noble, lonely Deirdre of a voice, a heroine sacrificed in a far exalted temple, the wraith of a thousand-years-gone love mindlessly calling through the tall glooms of the etheric world. I was still walking at sunrise, and when I felt like finding somewhere to sleep I was climbing into a small valley in the Pennines. The road had come to an end and a track climbed beside the untidy stream. It crossed it on a bridge, and just beyond was a caravan, abandoned, with flat tires. A mattress lay outside in the rain, a cushion was on the rocks under the bridge. Inside the caravan, on the table, a newspaper dated six months before was held down by two mugs. On the seat, bread was scattered by birds; the curtains slid to and fro in the wind; a coil of steel cable and a pickax lay on the floor, a crash helmet in the cupboard; on the ground were three heaps of new bricks and sand, and on the step a cartridge of lipstick.

Out in the Santa Monica Mountains they held a Renayssance Fayre. I had my caricature drawn by a quicker and simpler strolling artist than I. A hippie stood in one place all day, *gone*. I drew the profile of *Homo americanus*, standing at a fence overlooking an open-air theater; when he turned round, or walked, I had to circle him and get on the other side unobtrusively to finish my sketch, since I am incapable of mentally reversing an image. He noticed me holding my pencil and pretending to look elsewhere; said, "Looking for sketching material, are you?" and I said that sketching material was anything that stayed still. Everyone (even the bohemians) got into cars and drained away down to towns. I crossed a watercourse, stepping on newly hatched frogs the size of flies hopping over the scum in search of water; I pushed on to the top of the shallow valley, which was no more than a crease in dry parkland. Thinking about something else, I pitched my tent, which I didn't need to use at this season.

I hadn't even had time to go to sleep properly when I woke, with the conviction that someone had followed me up the valley, stepped right up to the tent, but hesitated and gone away again. I pictured her as carrying nothing in her hands, and shivering. I almost knocked the tent down around me. I stood up, looking in all directions by the very clear starlight. I felt that there was a cry over the whole landscape, though I couldn't quite hear it— high, light blue, cool, deathly, female, with the quality of a steel knife.

Last night, my lord, our love was red,   (4)
Tonight the very green of spring.
Would you that I conceive a bird?
Then but into my eyelid sing.
Unto my lord was born
Dolour and a daughter,
And, in one casket, a word
Burning, compressed, of slaughter.
When swearwords all are sent
Down to a swearwords' hell
The one word I bore for you
Will not fare you well.
My faithful name calls for you
As the river calls the rain.
At the stilling of all torrents
We two shall bed again.

karezza

Beta Capricorni said, "You know how I loathe the thought of having a child, but if the time ever comes when you say 'Goodbye, I'm going far away, I'll never see you again,' then I may decide I'd like your child as a memento." I smiled (at "if").

The time came, and I reminded her of what she had said. She had decided, yes. So for that last night we went into the room, shutting no door against the child.

While she was stripping, she didn't seem to change her mind. While she was lying down, she didn't seem to change her mind. While she was admitting me, she didn't seem to change her mind. But when I began to move in her, she changed her mind. But now there wasn't anything we could use.

"Keep still," she said.

We kept still all night.

This is the *Karezza*, which for those who can succeed in it is higher than any delight they have ever known. It is not itself delight, but what it is I cannot say.

After several hours I said, "There's no way of ending except the usual way. I know that isn't a very good reason for orgasm, but it's the main one. We have to end somehow."

"There will be no end," she said. "I'm casting a spell on you so that this will go on all your life. Now don't speak any more."

And so the hours that came after were the *Karezza* of

speech. The mind travels without limit when it is certain that nobody will speak and when the body has some pattern of action or inaction from which it need not diverge. Thus while walking over moor or desert I thrive in absolute loneliness, and think: "Could anything make it better? Only female against me and around me." But if she may speak, my mind is recalled and shrinks back into me; and if I move, there will be an end.

There are legends of books written in *Karezza;* of lovers who waited in *Karezza* for death.

Since then, I have, as if still walking in a dream of the *Karezza,* lusted and yearned away even more of my time, but that would no doubt have been the development, spell or no spell.

. . . what is it like to have blood kin? How do you really know your mother?

Can I only know through my daughter?

Suppose one day I met my own sister. She might be conservative, devout, stay-at-home, practical, sentimental—in every way I can name my opposite. Yet I would feel her immutable mannerisms from within . . .

folk song of the nation of one

The Nation of One has no national anthem, but it has forty-three songs (some translated from poems of other nations) and, at latest count, three hundred and eighty-eight musical themes. (The precision of the numbers is false, since many could be grouped, many subdivided.)

Since the nation is nomadic, always constrained to the duple rhythm of the feet, one would expect marching tunes, but they are few. Instead, increasingly, the tunes and the pure rhythms have come to be without cyclic beat. They are in irregular bars, or debatable bars, or no bars at all. Usually this fact comes as a surprise, being only discovered in the attempt to write the theme down.

One theory is that it is because the feet of the nation do not make a sound. This theory is inadequate, because the alternate retrieval of the thighs is as influential as any sound.

I shall give just one specimen. It has become the most famous among the nation. It is believed in the nation to be the most beautiful tune in the world.

It is believed that, sung quietly, heard in heads where there is anything of human organization, this tune is capable of engendering tenderness and stopping wars. Carried on a small flute across a gravelly parade ground, murmured by an anxious crowd, it quelled violence and decided the president of the nation to resign. It brings melancholy rather than peace; having no beat, it leads to no posthypnotic suggestion.

This is on a keyless stave used in the Nation of One; as
written elsewhere, it would have to be in a particular
key, such as:

It was at first called "The Garden," because the last
three notes of its second phrase have the resonance of a
garden in the early morning. Then it was called "Beth-
Eden" (the name of a woman and of an ancient kingdom
on the Euphrates) because it became a song with words
including those. Then, because there could never be enough
words and because it should not be limited to those words,
the words were stripped away and it became again a tune
only.

It has one chief variation, and twenty-two other sub-
stitutions of pitches, times, or phrases, giving a total of
28,144 permutations all of a simple kind, and there are
five related tunes which may be used as interludes. All
this was discovered only because tune and variants were
written down at various times in various countries, and
when the writings were put together they were found to be
different. It seems that this is melodic material which rami-
fies while one is not watching it, and which therefore is
probably still ramifying.

What is the nation to do with a tune that has at least
28,144 forms? They do not know, but meanwhile they do

not limit it even into a symphony. They prescribe no instrumentation for it, and take no copyright on it, in the hope that if left to time it will gradually achieve all the incarnations it deserves.

To begin with, it should be repeated a thousand times purely on the flute, without change, and then one may begin to treat its variants likewise, and after that one may begin to think of trying other instruments to it or words.

proposal to walk round the world

". . . a frozen corpse, set up at a crossroads, one arm pointing east—'Omsk, five hundred miles' . . . "

This was an old artillery sergeant narrating, and as I fought off sleep (I was the barman, and no army regulations would have saved me if I had tried to close the bar at midnight on a Saturday), my mouth-lined mind sank into its spiral of phrases—"Carcasses in the Caucasus. And Make Thy Frozen People Joyful. Our Father Which Art in Law. And Doeth begat Hath and Hath begat Forthwith and Forthwith begat Thenceforth . . ."

I will walk round the world, if I get some support, and if someone points the way.

Greet for me, Shanglu, the hard angels of nomadsland,
Quartzcragland, rockknuckleland, the vulture's hegemony, the spark in the sand;
Culve the chalk duchy, drift with the deer tribe, make mansions of thickets,
Hunt rivermark poplars, or dwell by a well with two plane trees.
Ground from here to my home is too tired for my burden.
Mazed line ends in a street that could well not have been.

(*Footnote:* Shanglu—Qashang Khan Ghalzai—is my double, whom I met in the town of Qandahar.)